JUDGING HUNTERS AND HUNTER SEAT EQUITATION

Now completely revised and updated, *Judging Hunters and Hunter Seat Equitation* is still the only single written source on how to judge hunter show competitions (under saddle classes, hunter classes over fences, conformation, and hunter seat equitation on the flat and over fences). Although the *AHSA Rule Book* is used as a basic guideline, it does not include the numerous details about performance that come into play when a person is judging.

Anna Jane White-Mullin recognizes the importance of addressing in print the questions she hears continually asked by judges and competitors. In this revised and updated edition, now in paperback, both audiences will find valuable explanations of what judges look for and the training methods necessary to accomplish the desired results. The more than 100 photographs of correct and incorrect positions of horses and riders will sharpen the eyes of judges and will serve as a self-correcting device for competitors. Also included are examples of judges' cards to provide further insight into what judges look for.

Anna Jane White-Mullin has been involved with horses for 33 years as a rider, teacher, and AHSA registered judge. She is also the author of *Winning: A Training and Showing Guide for Hunter Seat Riders*, which *The Chronicle of the Horse* called "thorough and well-organized" and which leading trainer Frank Madden hailed as "a unique tool to assist us in keeping our systems innovative."

By the same author

WINNING
A Training and Showing Guide for Hunter Seat Riders

JUDGING HUNTERS AND HUNTER SEAT EQUITATION

A Comprehensive Guide for Exhibitors and Judges

New and Revised Edition

ANNA JANE WHITE-MULLIN

Trafalgar Square Publishing

NORTH POMFRET, VERMONT

With love I dedicate this book to my parents
Mr. and Mrs. A. O. White, Jr.
and to my husband
Neil Dennis Mullin

In Chapter 1, all drawings by Sharon Ashby are reproduced courtesy of Equine Practice Magazine, *from D. V. Shively, D.V.M., "Equine-English Dictionary: Part II— Locomotion (Ways of Going)," vol. 4, no. 8, p. 17.*

In Chapter 3, all drawings by Sharon Ashby are reproduced courtesy of Equine Practice Magazine, *from D. V. Shively, D.V.M., "Equine-English Dictionary: Part 1—Standing Conformation," vol. 4, no. 5, pp. 10–20 and 25–27; and "Equine-English Dictionary: Part III—Lameness," vol. 4, no. 10, pp. 31–40.*

First published in 1984 by Arco Publishing, Inc.
This revised edition published in 1993 by
Trafalgar Square Publishing
North Pomfret, Vermont 05053

Library of Congress Cataloging-in-Publication Data
White-Mullin, Anna Jane.
Judging hunters and hunter seat equitation : a comprehensive guide for exhibitors and judges / Anna Jane White-Mullin. — New and rev. ed.
        p. cm.
  Includes index.
  ISBN 0-943955-80-7 : $19.95
  1. Hunter classes—Judging. 2. Hunter seat equitation division—Judging. I. Title.
SF296.H86W45 1993
798.2—dc20   93-3039
                              CIP

Printed in the United States of America
10 9 8 7 6 5 4 3 2 1

CONTENTS

3   CONFORMATION CLASSES 58

ACKNOWLEDGMENTS

Revised Edition

I would like to thank J. A. "Bucky" Reynolds for providing information for the added section on Model and Breeding Classes and Stephen O. Hawkins for editing the revised chapter on the Judge's Card.

First Edition

Special thanks to William C. Steinkraus for his advice and guidance during the last year of this project.

I would like to express my gratitude to the following horsemen who read portions of the text prior to publication and offered their valuable opinions:

Under-Saddle Classes and *Hunter Classes Over Fences*
    Earl "Red" Frazier, Stephen O. Hawkins, Daniel P. Lenehan, and George H. Morris
Conformation Classes
    A. Eugene Cunningham, Dr. Charles W. Crowe, Earl "Red" Frazier, Stephen O. Hawkins, Dr. Milton D. Kingsbury, George H. Morris, and Kenneth M. Wheeler
Equitation on the Flat and *Equitation Over Fences*
    Stephen O. Hawkins and George H. Morris
Dressage Movements in Tests 1–18
    Andrew B. DeSzinay and Col. Donald W. Thackeray

And to the judges who contributed their comments and systems of scoring to the final chapter:
    Stephen O. Hawkins, Chrystine W. Jones, Daniel P. Lenehan, George H. Morris, and Michael O. Page.

My thanks also to those who helped me in other ways during the past two years of working on the book:
    Phyllis and Inez Pennington of Pennington Galleries

and Frank Brenner, Frank Madden, Bill Cooney, Clea Newman, George Lindemann, Jr., Suzie Richburg, Dr. M. J. Shively, Sharon Ashby, *Equine Practice* magazine, *Practical Horseman* magazine, Deborah Lyons, Budd Studio, Kathy Paxson, Anne Allen Cheatham, Sally Salter, Sheila Ellison, Laura Kent, Mary Elizabeth Kent, Dan Bowers, Linda McFarland, Ann Dionne, Mr. and Mrs. Claude Rankin, Mrs. Haywood Nelms, Ken Cartmill, Phil Winningham, Helen Pyron, Jenno Topping, Tim Kees, Tosca Kocken, Paul Valliere, Francesca Mazella, and Linda Kossick.

JUDGING HUNTERS
AND HUNTER SEAT
EQUITATION

PREFACE

While attending an AHSA judges' clinic in Charlottesville, Virginia, several years ago, I realized the participants were asking many questions that had never been addressed in print. Although we have the *AHSA Rule Book* to use as a basic guideline, it does not include the thousands of details about performance that come into play when a person is judging a class.

Much has been written on the subject of how to ride, but nothing has been written concerning how committing errors in the show ring affects the relative placement of horses and riders. By providing this information, I hope to answer many of the questions posed by judges, riders, and trainers and to standardize judging practices on a national basis for under-saddle classes, hunter classes over fences, conformation, and hunter seat equitation on the flat and over fences.

Oral transmission of this information is impossible in many areas, since there are only a few parts of the country where the sport has become sophisticated enough that correct information would be passed on through conversation or day to day experience. I believe this book can be beneficial to those judges, riders, and trainers who want to increase their knowledge but who do not have the personal contacts or the financial means to go outside their areas for the length of time necessary to significantly further their education.

Beyond the transmission of specific information, I am interested in the potentially positive effect *Judging Hunters and Hunter Seat Equita-*

1

tion can have on participants' attitudes toward horse shows. I believe, for the betterment of the sport, there should be a written explanation of how horses and riders are judged so competitors will realize that there are set standards for judging and that they can have faith in the integrity of the sport.

Finally, I feel that a person has accomplished nothing if he is only self-serving in his goals. While my study of various aspects of horse sports has brought personal enjoyment for twenty-five years, it will only bring a sense of fulfillment if I can benefit someone else by sharing what I have learned.

Anna Jane White-Mullin

PREFACE TO THE SECOND EDITION

Judging Hunters and Hunter Seat Equitation has been revised to reflect changes in Tests 1–19 since 1984, provide information on Breeding classes, and give more information on Numerical Scoring. The changes in Tests 1–19 are minimal, consisting mostly of a change in the order of the tests listed in the *AHSA Rule Book*.

The added information on Breeding classes is a result of the current requirement that judges hold a separate card to judge the Breeding Division, a requirement that did not exist when the book was first published. The standards for judging horses' conformation remain the same as in the Conformation Division, but the emphasis on the jog is increased in Model and Breeding classes as a major indicator of the horses' performance ability, since the judge does not have a chance to see these horses work.

The chapter on the Judge's Card reflects a more widespread use of the Numerical System of scoring. This system was once reserved for the largest shows in the country, but now small shows often hold "mini-Classics" that require the judge to make his score public. Even when judges are not required to hold up their scores, it is advisable for them to practice this system so that they will feel comfortable using it.

I intend to keep this book as current as possible and hope that you will find the text beneficial, whether you are a judge, coach, or rider.

Anna Jane White-Mullin

FOREWORD

In 1917, when the American Horse Shows Association (AHSA) was founded, the sport of showing horses was not complicated. Most shows were held in open fields, and the exhibitors were residents of areas near the competitions. As the years passed, however, more and more people began showing and because of transportation improvements, exhibitors began to be drawn from greater distances. Gradually, showing grew into a nationwide sport. Of all the divisions recognized by the AHSA, the area of greatest growth has been Hunter and Hunter Seat Equitation. Since 1955, these divisions have increased at a phenomenal rate, and the procedures now necessary to produce winners involve prolonged training of both horse and rider.

Exhibitors and trainers from the larger, more sophisticated stables around the country know the rules and, in general, know what the judges are looking for. Nonetheless, there are many fine points covered in this book which even the most knowledgeable horsemen and horsewomen will find helpful.

For those who are not in this category, the author has produced a work that should be studied seriously. There are many valuable explanations of what judges look for and of the training methods necessary to accomplish these desired results. The detailed explanations should be especially beneficial to young riders and trainers, who often do not comprehend why one round wins over another and how one small facet of a performance can make the difference between first and second places in a class.

The author's background well qualifies her as an authority in this capacity. She started riding at age five and went on to win many national awards, including bronze, silver, and gold medals in the United States Equestrian Team classes. In 1971, she was winner of the Alfred B. Maclay Finals at Madison Square Garden, triumphing over 120 other top-rank finalists. With her outstanding junior hunter, Rivet, she won championships at every major horse show at which they exhibited, including Madison Square Garden, Harrisburg, Washington, and the Florida circuit shows. Currently an AHSA registered judge, she teaches junior and amateur-owner riders at her stable, Bellerophon, in Gadsden, Alabama.

Stephen O. Hawkins
New York City

INTRODUCTION

In the old days, and I mean twenty-five years ago, two types of judges were invited to horse shows. Those most often asked were very socially accepted people, who—it was hoped—also knew something about horses. Contrary to belief, lots of those men and women were exceptional horsemen and horsewomen; they had been brought up all their lives to participate in many different horse sports. Not quite so frequently, the others who were asked to judge were local professionals who were also (almost) socially acceptable. These men (rarely women) were usually good, solid horsemen of the old school who had worked their way up to prominence. Because of the social whirl surrounding even a one-day show (let alone the long major shows!), "party manners" were a prerequisite to an invitation.

Nowadays things are different. Horse showing has become a very serious, competitive, and expensive sport. The social aspect, while still evident, has definitely taken a back seat to the game at hand. It is for this reason that show management, though still prone to ask the fun friend, is under a great deal of pressure to invite a "popular" judge. This man or woman is conscientious, knows his job well, and keeps more of the people happy more of the time than some of the less "popular" judges. The big problem in judging today is nobody's fault. The most talented and progressive teachers, trainers, and riders are too busy showing to have much time to judge. The judges, therefore, are sometimes just a bit behind the newest and, perhaps, the best ways of doing things. I say "perhaps" because sound and progressive techniques can often be misrepresented, misunderstood, or exaggerated. In this instance, some of the old beats the new.

Three things are expected of judges. First, that they be knowledgeable of the rules and of their subject. Second, that they be "good bookkeepers" in handling a judge's card. And third, that they be scrupulously honest. Honesty, of course, is strictly a matter of character. It is simply the person at hand, and that is that. However, knowledge and bookkeeping can and should always be improved.

Experience is a great teacher. But, my goodness, it takes a long time! Clinics and seminars are fine, except that they last only a day or two and they are few and far between. But now we have a book to help us, and a comprehensive book it is. We can all hope to learn more quickly than ever before by studying this wonderful text on judging.

Over the years, the sport of showing hunters has changed a great deal. We used to see lots of middleweight and heavyweight horses, both thoroughbred and half-bred. These horses had lots of bone and strong quarters, were good gallopers, and could often jump a big fence. Today the overwhelming number of horses showing as hunters are lightweights. Although these horses often are "pretty," move well, and jump low fences in good form, they generally don't have the substance to do too much more. Funnily enough, through the importation of European warmbloods, we are again seeing bigger horses coming back into the hunter ring and competing successfully. The pendulum swings!

Hunters go differently today, too. Up until the mid-1950s, the emphasis was on pace and a brilliant, long jumping effort. Most of the horses were not schooled; they bordered on being runaways. Woe to the fellow on a mediocre jumper who came in "wrong." He usually stood on his head! Horses in under-saddle classes went on loose reins, cutting their corners. Contact and bending? What on earth were they talking about!

Today we want balance and precision. Speed? Why, that is hardly noticed. Eight jumps exactly alike, working on straight lines and bent turns is what wins the blue ribbon. The schooling of horses has finally come into its own. Time marches on and things get better. Now it's the "short option," not your life!

The Hunter Seat Equitation division has changed dramatically, too. Of course, the training of a rider always has to precede the training of his horse. The animal can do only what the rider asks him to do. Again, the big turning point came in the first half of the 1950s. While the forward seat has been around for half a century, few riders were among the "enlightened" until after the Second World War. Heels down, eyes up, lean forward, follow the mouth were techniques foreign to those "seat-of-the-panters" who only knew the old "hunting" seat. The sixties and seventies saw the influence of dressage. And the forward seat can now be considered a balanced seat—neither too forward nor too backward—and most classic in appearance. Truly we have a unique American style coupled with marvelous control. And this is due in large part to our equitation division.

Where will judging and showing go from here?—not likely to anything radically new. Horses will be horses, and riders will be riders, and good sound basics will prevail. We'll always have to be on guard against the trendy, the mannered, and the exaggerated. After all, only the horse will really know. And he'll always tell us…if we were born to listen.

George H. Morris
Pittstown, New Jersey

NOTE TO THE READER

The photographic examples that accompany the text were chosen from files of horse-show *negatives*, with my having no knowledge of horse or rider identity. These moments captured on film are intended for instructional use only and in no way indicate the overall ability of rider and horse.

Throughout the book, I will often "pin the class" by placing the errors discussed in their order of severity. In every case, I am assuming the horses being pinned are the only horses in the class, for many of the faults that will be placed would keep the horses that committed them out of the ribbons in most competitions.

1

UNDER-SADDLE CLASSES

The Ideal Horse

The *AHSA Rule Book* states that horses being shown in under-saddle classes "should be obedient, alert, responsive, and move freely." Let's begin by examining the ideal horse, one that exhibits all of these qualities.

The ideal horse moves freely, stretching for long, athletic steps instead of taking short, high steps. Viewed from the side, it will be seen to swing its legs close to the ground and reach to the full length of its stride at all gaits (Figs. 1-1A, B, C). Observed from the front or hind perspective, it travels squarely.

This ideal animal is "on the bit" and in a balanced frame at all gaits. It is neither "overflexed," with its head forced behind the vertical, nor is it strung out on loose reins with no frame at all; rather, it is positioned between these two extremes. The ideal frame for each horse depends on its particular conformation, disposition, and locomotion (Figs. 1-2A, B, C). Since "light contact with the horse's mouth" is required by the *Rule Book*, any horse being shown on loose reins in an under-saddle class must be penalized heavily for not meeting class requirements.

Our ideal horse keeps a constant rhythm at each gait and maintains appropriate forward momentum into the downward transitions, making them smooth rather than abrupt. Its hindquarters, well under it, demonstrate continuous forward impulsion. On the corners of the ring the

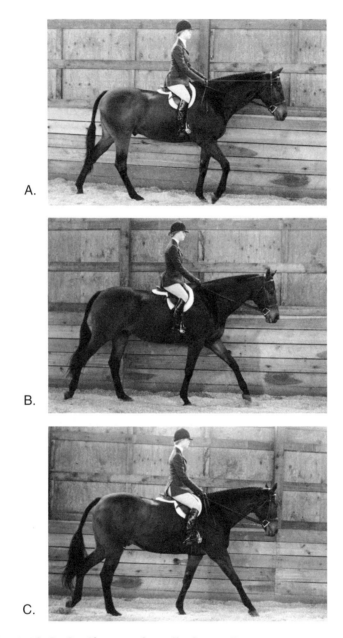

A.

B.

C.

Figs. 1-1A, B, C—Shown at the walk, this excellent mover skims its toe just above the ground (A), stretches its foreleg to reach for the maximum length of the step (B), and fully extends the leg slightly before the hoof touches the footing (C). Photographs by Frank Brenner

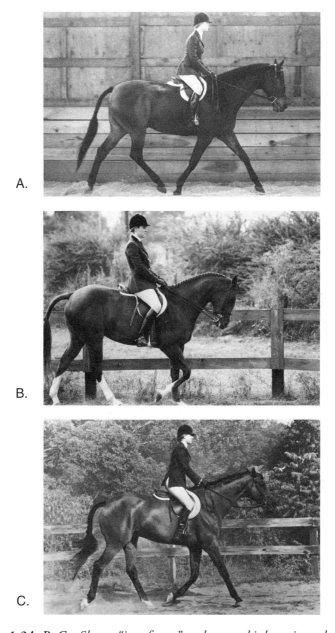

Figs. 1-2A, B, C—Shown "in a frame" at the trot, this horse is on the bit and moving with impulsion (A). In contrast, the chestnut horse is being "overflexed" at the walk, so that its head is incorrectly forced behind the vertical (B). At the opposite extreme is the bay horse that travels "strung out" on loose reins at the trot (C). Photograph A by Frank Brenner/B by Dan Bowers/C by Images of Rhode Island

horse is bent from head to tail in the direction of travel, and on the straight sides of the ring, its body is straight (Figs. 1-3A, B).

This ideal animal is prompt, yet smooth, in both upward and downward transitions. It is relaxed, but not dull, and is willing to go forward. Attentive, but calm, it doesn't become excited or buck and play if you call for a hand gallop. A pleasant expression and ears pointed forward indicate the animal's cooperative attitude.

Now the ideal is established, let's look at a variety of performance faults you may see while judging and consider their relative penalties.

Unsafe Performance

Unsafe behavior receives the heaviest penalties in this as in every phase of hunter seat riding that is judged on quality of performance. The horse

Figs. 1-3A, B—Compare a horse that is not bent on a corner (A) to one that is correctly bent in the direction of travel (B), and notice the difference in balance, field of vision, and forward momentum. Photographs by A. O. White, Jr.

that bolts (runs off) with its rider and the horse that rears are most dangerous. Less serious offenders, but still receiving heavy penalties, are the horse that bucks and the animal that shies. These forms of bad behavior are severely penalized because they endanger the rider and can cause harm to other competitors in the class.

The only exception you might consider in this area would be a horse that bucks or shies mildly under "extenuating circumstances." For instance, if an otherwise well-behaved horse gives a little buck when another competitor's horse runs into it from behind, you might forgive this behavioral fault; but you should penalize severely a horse that lets out a walloping buck with no apparent provocation. Similarly, you should penalize heavily a tense horse that goes around the ring looking for trouble, shying in response to every sound and movement, or even shying at inanimate objects. However, you can be lenient with an animal that shies slightly when someone parked by the railing inconsiderately starts a noisy engine just as the horse is passing by.

In judging performance, everything is relative. The little buck or small shy might end up being a deciding factor in top company, but a horse's normal reaction to an unusual situation should not necessarily exclude the animal from the ribbons.

Length of Stride

Less heavily penalized than the serious behavioral problems, but still considered major faults, are flaws in the animal's locomotion. A horse with short, high-action steps lacks the athletic appearance we desire in a hunter and is often a bumpy, unpleasant ride. This "poor mover" should place only when a small number of entries or a lack of quality competition leaves you no choice (Fig. 1-4).

Preferable to this is a "fair mover," a horse that has either a long stride and high action or a short stride and low action—that is, its way of moving is good in some respects, but it still has a major locomotion flaw (Figs. 1-5A, B).

Surpassing the fair mover in quality is the "good mover." This horse displays a long enough, low enough stride to be in the ribbons in moderately stiff competition, or to place in higher competition if the better movers commit major faults, but it lacks the exceptionally long, flowing stride that marks a top-quality horse. A "good mover" and an "excellent mover" are virtually indistinguishable in photographs, since the main

Fig. 1-4—This "poor mover" has mostly upward motion at the trot; its hocks and knees display excess vertical action. This type of chunky horse, built short in the body and upright in the joints, is usually a poor mover. Notice how the horse's short, upright neck adds to the impression of extreme vertical motion in this picture. Photograph by Pennington Galleries

difference between the two is the extra flowing motion the "excellent mover" has which cannot be captured when you stop the action, even in sequential photographs. However, when judging a class, it will be obvious to you which are the "good movers" that travel long and low, and which are the "excellent movers" that travel long, low, and with such ease that they seem to float across the footing.

An "excellent mover" is the picture of elegance as it swings its limbs forward with each step and stretches for the ground. This quality animal has minimal upward action and maximum forward thrust of the limbs (Fig. 1-6; also see Figs. 1-1A, B, C and Fig. 1-2A). In the forelegs, the knee and fetlock joints hardly bend, so that in all gaits the hooves travel close to the ground; the animal is said to move with a "daisy-cutting" motion. The hind legs stretch forward with each step, maintaining solid impulsion at each gait and throughout the transitions. The hock joints

A.

B.

Figs. 1-5A, B—Although this horse has an adequately long stride (A), the upward action of its knees and hocks (B), makes the animal only a "fair mover." As in Fig. 1-4, the horse's high head carriage accentuates its locomotion faults. Photographs by Dan Bowers

Fig. 1-6—A long stride and straightness of the limbs in motion are shown in this photograph of an excellent mover at the canter. It is obvious from the secure position of the rider that the horse accepts the aids of the hand, seat, and leg. Notice that the animal's head is on the vertical, the greatest degree of flexion possible without incurring a penalty. Photograph by Frank Brenner

open and close with a fluid movement that allows the horse to reach forward with its hind legs in flowing, athletic steps. Lesser movers may appear stiff in the hocks, take short steps with the hind legs, and trail their rear ends; in contrast, an excellent mover shows smooth, low, long, and powerful steps in its hind end, "engaging" its hocks while working at each gait.

Appropriate Frame

Besides noting length of stride, consider the horse's general carriage or "frame." A strung-out horse that moves with its head poking out at the end of a loose rein is most unattractive when compared to a horse that has been put on the bit and is carrying itself in a balanced frame, with hocks well under its body at each step. You are not looking for a horse to be so collected that it could perform a piaffe, but neither do you want to pin a horse that hacks quietly only on a loose rein, for the rider's avoidance of

A.

B.

Figs. 1-7A, B—*This horse's well-carried ears, pleasant expression, and lengthy stride make a nice picture (A), but the loose reins and the muscularity of the underside of its neck suggest a problem. As you can see, with even the slightest rein contact, this horse begins to raise its head in an effort to escape being on the bit (B). The muscular lower neck confirms that this is a chronic problem. Photographs by Dan Bowers*

Fig. 1-8—Stiffening its neck and jaw, the horse is hanging on the rider's hands, "pulling" against her rather than willingly submitting to the pressure of her aids. The opposite of pulling is "dropping behind the bit," during which the horse draws its head toward the vertical to evade hand pressure, leaving the rider no means of communication through the reins (see Fig. 4-24A). Photograph by Images of Rhode Island

putting the horse on the bit suggests that the animal becomes excited, resistant, or evasive when contact is established with its mouth (Figs. 1-7A, B). A horse in under-saddle classes should accept the bit and go to it willingly, rather than hang on the rider's hands or duck behind the bit to escape pressure (Fig. 1-8).

Body Straightness

After you have looked for length of stride and general carriage from the side, move to an area of the ring where you can view the horses in the class from either a front or a hind perspective in order to check the straightness of their bodies in motion. An animal that doesn't move straight should be penalized, since lack of straightness limits the horse as an athlete and often leads to unsoundness.

However, a horse that doesn't move straight should be penalized less severely than a short-strided animal (unless the lack of straightness is causing lameness during the class). The reason for this is that a horse with a long, smooth stride may not move completely straight, but as long as its lack of straightness doesn't cause lameness, the animal will have an adequate stride to make a smooth round over fences. The choppy, short-strided horse, on the other hand, may move straight, but it will never have the athletic ability to turn in a smooth, flowing trip, and its short, uncomfortable gait will make it unpleasant to ride.

Common Locomotion Faults

Any deviation from straightforward locomotion should be penalized. For instance, some horses move crookedly throughout their bodies, with their hind feet and their forefeet traveling on separate tracks (Fig. 1-9).

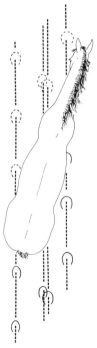

Fig. 1-9—A horse that moves crooked ("dog-style") is often a sufferer from trochanteric bursitis. The animal shifts toward the sound side since the stride on the affected side is shortened. Drawing by Sharon Ashby

Since this crookedness pervades the horse's every effort on the flat and over fences, you should penalize it severely.

Horses that do not move crookedly throughout their bodies may still have a locomotion problem because of the turn of their legs—either the entire leg or the leg from the knee or fetlock down. The worst fault resulting from these structural problems is "plaiting": the animal places one foot in front of the other so that the hooves on opposite sides of the body track the same path, instead of the right feet tracking one path and the left feet tracking another (Fig. 1-10). Most often found in horses with base-narrow, toe-out conformation, plaiting is heavily penalized because it can cause stumbling and result in injury to the horse and/or rider.

A lesser fault in locomotion is "winging," in which the horse brushes past the inside of one leg with the hoof of the opposite leg and places the foot outside the imaginary line from shoulder to ground on which the hoof should land during travel (Fig. 1-11). Associated with toe-out conformation, winging is penalized because it can cause trauma in one or both of the legs involved, first from the brushing of the hoof against the opposite leg, and second from the excess pressure the horse places on the inside of one leg as it sets the hoof down too far to the outside of the correct path.

"Paddling" is another locomotion fault seen in under-saddle classes. Here the horse swings its foot to the outside of the imaginary line from shoulder to ground on which the hoof should be traveling and places the hoof to the inside of that line, causing excess weight to be thrust upon the outside of the foot (Fig. 1-12). Associated with toe-in conformation, paddling shows a lack of proper weight distribution on the leg and a lack of straightforward thrust of the horse's legs. However, paddling poses no danger of one leg interfering with another, so you should penalize it less severely than plaiting or winging.

Rhythm, Transitions, and Bending

Rhythm is another aspect of performance to consider in judging under-saddle classes. The animal that maintains a constant rhythm at its gaits is more attractive than one that looks as though it will "die out" and break gait or one that seems to be "on the muscle," gaining momentum with every stride. You should notice a horse's rhythm during the walk as well as during the other gaits, for too often judges as well as riders regard the walk as a "time out." It is important that competitors who do try to show

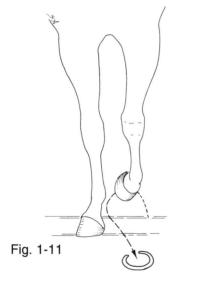

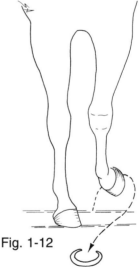

Fig. 1-10—*In plaiting ("singletracking"), the horse's front feet are placed directly, or almost directly, in front of each other. Plaiting often causes stumbling and is heavily penalized in under-saddle classes. Drawing by Sharon Ashby*

Fig. 1-11

Fig. 1-12

Fig. 1-11 (left)—*Winging ("wing-in") is penalized for the excess pressure it puts on the inside of the leg as the hoof is placed to the outside of the proper track and for the interference to the opposite leg which often results from moving in this manner. Drawing by Sharon Ashby*

Fig. 1-12 (right)—*Paddling ("wing-out") causes unequal weight distribution on the leg as the foot is placed to the inside of the proper track. However, it is not as heavily penalized as winging or plaiting because paddling does not cause interference. Drawing by Sharon Ashby*

their mounts in a solid cadence at the walk receive credit for the quality of their performance at this often "forgotten gait."

The rhythm of the gaits should not be broken abruptly by downward transitions that look as though the horse is "slamming on the brakes." Both upward and downward transitions should be as smooth as possible, with a prompt and fluid transition being preferable to a prompt but abrupt one.

Besides maintaining steady rhythm in the gaits and performing smooth transitions, a horse in under-saddle classes should be bent in the direction of travel around the corners of the ring and move straight on the straight sides. A horse that negotiates corners improperly—with its head turned to the outside—should be penalized heavily, for its lack of correct bending jeopardizes its balance, limits its field of vision, and in most cases causes the animal to shorten its stride because it loses some of its forward momentum as it leans to the inside of the ring (see Figs. 1-3A, B).

Summary

After you have weeded out any horses that display behavioral problems (bolting, rearing, bucking, et cetera), or commit major performance errors (breaking gait or picking up the wrong lead), consider each remaining animal's action of the limbs, length of stride, and frame. Then look for alignment problems, such as crooked movement throughout the body, plaiting, winging, or paddling. After you have used the criteria detailed above to select the horses of the best quality in the class, consider each animal's overall performance: its willingness to go forward in a definite cadence at all gaits, whether or not it was bent properly on the corners of the ring, the smoothness of its upward and downward transitions, and the general presentation its rider has made of it during the class. Next, pin the class accordingly.

Although you may call for a hand gallop in under-saddle classes (unless the class specifications do not allow it), this test often does more harm than good, for it only takes one uncontrollable animal to ruin the performances of a number of other competitors. In calling for the hand gallop, you risk losing your top horses and may find yourself in the embarrassing position of pinning several "clunkers." I believe this is the reason the hand gallop is being seen less and less each year at major shows;

Fig. 1-13—At the hand gallop, the rider is in two-point position: legs are on the horse's sides while the seat is held out of the saddle. By adding leg pressure, the rider causes the horse to lengthen its stride and increase its pace to a controlled, three-beat "gallop in hand" at 14 to 16 mph. Photograph by Suzie Richburg

many judges have found that the risk of the test outweighs any benefit it may provide in determining the best horse.

However, if you do decide to hand-gallop the horses, ask no more than eight at a time to perform the test. Look for animals that increase their pace beyond a canter (10 to 12 mph) to a controlled gallop (14 to 16 mph), while demonstrating the features desired during the other gaits—especially long, low strides and relaxed obedience. If a horse becomes dangerously fast or switches leads during this test, it should be dropped to the bottom of the class. Consider the condition and size of the arena before calling for this test; slippery footing or an overly small ring can threaten the safety of horse and rider at the increased pace of a hand gallop.

When properly performing this test, the horse calmly increases its pace, lengthens its stride, and remains on the bit without fighting the rider's hands (Fig. 1-13). Horses that "suck back" and refuse to increase pace in resistance to the rider's legs should be penalized heavily for not performing the test. Animals that become excited and pull against their riders or that buck and play rather than remain calm are also heavily penalized. Although the *Rule Book* requires rein contact during all under-saddle tests, following the hand gallop the rider may allow the horse to move back into line on loose reins to demonstrate the horse's relaxation following this test.

2

HUNTER CLASSES OVER FENCES

JUMPING FORM

The Ideal Hunter

What are the components of an ideal performance in a hunter class over fences? First, the ideal horse will meet each fence at the correct takeoff spot for a perfect arc over the obstacle. Its jump will be "snappy" and athletic, with the forearms held at or above a parallel line to the ground, the joints of the front legs tucked tightly in front of its chest, and the neck and back arched over the fence (Figs. 2-1A, B). It will begin its round at a pace suited to the size of the fences and sustain this pace for the entire trip, staying straight through its body when negotiating fences on a straight line and bending in the direction of travel on the corners of the ring.

That's the ideal, but in judging you rarely observe this flawless performance, so let's look at faults you may see while judging a hunter class over fences and consider the degree of penalty for each.

Form Faults Associated with Long Spots

The worst error in a class over fences is a "risky" fence in which the horse leaves the ground dangerously far from the base of the obstacle (Figs. 2-

A.

B.

Figs. 2-1A, B—*Viewed from the side, this animal demonstrates excellent form: knees held high and even, hooves tucked, and its topline forming a beautiful arc (A). Captured from a front view, this horse displays every aspect of an ideal hunter, from its superb form to its attentive, yet relaxed expression (B). Photographs by Pennington Galleries*

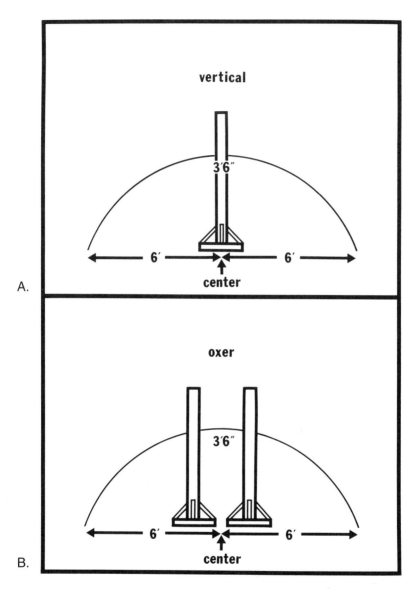

Figs. 2-2A, B—*The diagram shows the approximate proper takeoff distances at verticals (A) and oxers (B) measuring 3 feet 6 inches or higher. For fences under 3 feet 6 inches, the horse should leave the ground and land approximately 5 feet from the center of the fence. If a horse leaves the ground much farther away than these measurements, it could have a "risky" fence. Diagrams by the author*

2A, B). An animal that realizes it has left the ground too far from the base of a fence may try to put its feet back on the ground on the near side of the obstacle and crash through the fence; or a horse may flail its legs in an effort to propel itself in the air and barely clear the obstacle (Fig. 2-3). Another drastic alternative is "diving": the horse stretches its front legs so far forward in an effort to clear the rails that it appears to be diving toward the ground (Fig. 2-4). Any of these desperate actions should keep a horse out of the ribbons unless the class is so small or the trips so bad that you have no other choice.

"Reaching" and "cutting down" are less dangerous methods of dealing with a risky spot, but are still major faults. In "reaching," a milder form of diving, the horse tries to clear the obstacle by stretching its front legs forward—beyond their normal position in the air—often in a quick, frantic movement (Fig. 2-5). In "cutting down," the horse unfolds its legs early on the far side of the fence, landing closer to the center of the fence on the far side than its takeoff was to the center on the near side (Fig. 2-6). Cutting down demonstrates lack of scope, since a more ath-

Fig. 2-3—Flailing its legs to gain vital inches, this horse is struggling to avoid a crash. Photograph by Pennington Galleries

Fig. 2-4—*The outstretched forelegs show why this desperate attempt to clear the obstacle is called "diving." Photograph by Pennington Galleries*

Fig. 2-5—*Although the horse has achieved the peak of its arc, it has not gotten to the fence. By this time, the horse's girth should be directly above the rails. Notice the right forefoot beginning to "reach" to clear the obstacle. Photograph by Pennington Galleries*

Fig. 2-6—From the clumps of dislodged footing on the near side of the fence, you can see that the horse's takeoff spot was farther away from the obstacle than the place of landing will be. The downturned angle of the horse's body in the air—at the point at which the animal should be at the peak of its arc—is called "cutting down." Photograph by A. O. White, Jr.

letic horse in the same situation would leave from the long distance, make its arc higher than the size of the fence demanded (though appropriate to the takeoff spot), and land as far from the fence on the far side as it took off from the fence on the near side.

Unless the horse that cuts down also carries a rail to the ground with its hind feet, you should penalize this fault less severely than reaching. The reasoning is that in reaching, the horse risks catching its front limbs on the obstacle and possibly flipping over in the air. In cutting down, the horse risks catching its hind limbs on the obstacle—a fault that has much less potential danger for the rider and horse. (As a rule, front-end errors are more heavily penalized than hind-end errors.)

In a class consisting only of the horses mentioned, you would pin as follows: sixth, the horse that tried to put its feet back on the ground on the near side of the fence and crashed; fifth, the horse that flailed its legs but cleared the fence; fourth, the horse that dove over the fence; third, the horse that reached; and second, the one that cut down. The winner would be the athletic horse that compensated for the long spot with an even arc.

Form Faults Associated with Short Spots

When a horse leaves the ground from a spot too close to the fence—whether the rider has placed it there or the horse happened to meet that spot through lack of rider assistance—the animal should compensate for the deep spot by bringing its hocks well under its body on the takeoff stride and rocking backward slightly more than it would for a medium spot, so that its legs will be away from the rails. A talented, athletic horse will get its rider out of trouble this way, but a lazy or untalented one will hit the top of the fence with its front feet.

Even worse than the horse that doesn't mind touching the fence is the one that hangs its legs down toward the fence when placed at a deep spot. Not only is hanging visually unattractive, but it should be penalized severely for safety reasons: a horse that hangs its front legs could catch one or both of its forelimbs on the top of the obstacle and have a serious accident (Figs. 2-7A, B, C). Front and hind legs should be neatly tucked while jumping so there is no danger of the animal entangling itself in the rails. You should penalize a horse that hangs even if it doesn't touch the rails, for the *Rule Book* directs that "Judges must penalize unsafe jumping and bad form over fences, whether touched or untouched."

In judging only these horses that have taken off from deep spots, place third the horse that is lazy with its legs and hangs. Pin second the horse that remains in good form but has a front-end touch, and place first the horse that rocks back at takeoff and copes with its placement in an athletic manner.

Another form fault you may see when a horse meets a fence from a spot too deep is "propping." A horse that props appears to be pushing back from the fence during the approach to the obstacle and at takeoff, in an effort to get its front legs away from the rails (Figs. 2-8A, B). When a rider attempts to drive a horse past a reasonable takeoff spot, the horse may prop to set itself up to jump in good form despite the rider's signals. Propping may be caused also by a weak rider who allows the horse to slow down at every fence, so the animal becomes accustomed to making the smallest effort possible to get over the fences. In its slightest form, propping is not heavily penalized, for it is not a dangerous fault but only an

A.

B.

C.

Figs. 2-7A, B, C—"Hanging" is captured from a side view (A), front view (B), and an oblique view that shows why this fault can be dangerous (C). Photographs by Pennington Galleries

A.

B.

Figs. 2-8A, B—When a horse "props," its front feet hit the ground together at the last stride before takeoff, so that when captured on film, the animal appears to be stopping at the obstacle (A). Compare the horse that props with a horse that correctly leaves the ground with its front feet maintaining the normal stride sequence (B). Photographs by Linda McFarland

interruption in the horse's forward flow of energy at takeoff. However, if the horse chronically props, as in the case of the weak rider who lets the horse prop at every fence, the penalty should be great, for chronic propping is a manifestation of the horse's general unwillingness to go forward.

Other Form Faults

You may see other form faults while a horse is airborne, such as a horse that "lies on its side" by tilting in midair so that one of its sides is inclined toward the ground and the other toward the sky (Fig. 2-9). Penalize this fault severely, since it shows a marked lack of balance and can be quite

Fig. 2-9—"Lying on its side" aptly describes this horse's posture in the air. Notice the rider slipping toward the down-turned side of the animal. Photograph by Pennington Galleries

dangerous: if the rider's weight shifts radically toward the down side, the horse may be unable to land on its feet.

Less serious than inclining to one side is "twisting" over a fence, in which the horse remains upright in the air, but writhes during its flight path in order to let the front and hind limbs clear the fence (Fig. 2-10). A horse may twist for one of several reasons: an overfaced animal may be struggling to clear the fences; a horse with a physical disorder, such as a navicular or a back problem, may be incapable of a straight jumping effort; or a lazy horse placed at a deep spot may twist instead of rocking back on its hocks to clear an obstacle. Whatever its cause, twisting receives a severe penalty.

Fig. 2-10—This horse is "twisting" its front end to bring its legs over the rails. The probable cause is a deep takeoff spot, as indicated by the hind legs being very close to the fence. Photograph by Pennington Galleries

Minor Form Faults

The faults we have considered so far—hanging, diving, reaching, cutting down, lying on the side, and twisting—are serious enough to keep a horse out of the ribbons. Now we will consider less serious faults that will also affect your placement of horses in a class.

A horse with legs not folded tightly when it jumps shows "loose form" (Figs. 2-11A, B). You may end up pinning a horse with loose form in moderately stiff competition if everything else about its trip is top-notch and its legs are only loose, not dangling down from its shoulders as in hanging. However, in a good class of athletic jumpers and excellent movers, a horse with loose form will suffer in the pinning.

Another fault you may see over fences is a horse carrying its legs too close to each other or too far apart. Some horses' legs are so close together in the air that one hoof appears to be wrapped around the other, while other horses' legs are so wide apart that they display an expanse of chest between the forelegs while airborne (Figs. 2-12A, B). Neither leg position presents a threat to the rider's safety, so you only need to consider these faults in a class where the trips are so similar in quality that you must use style as the deciding factor.

Form of the Back and Neck

Form over fences does not depend entirely on the horse's use of its legs, but involves the back and neck as well. When we speak of a horse "using itself," we mean that the animal elevates its body in the air in an arched manner, so the back and neck look rounded rather than flat and stiff (Figs. 2-13A, B, C). An arched neck and back are signs of an athletic or "scopey" horse, and horses that have this athletic look accompanied by good leg formation should place above horses that have tightly folded legs and a flat appearance of the back.

An interesting observation was made by a professional horseman who said he found that horses that use their backs well often hang their legs, and horses that use their legs well are often flat in their backs. From his point of view, he preferred to own the horse that used its back well and was lazy with its legs, reasoning that an agile back shows good scope, and when the fences become higher, the horse will have to use its legs as well as its back to clear them and at such times will jump in good form. On

A.

B.

Figs. 2-11A, B—*The open knee and fetlock joints of this horse (A) should be marked "loose form." The animal's knees are just high enough not to be marked "hanging." Although the other horse (B) seems to be "reaching" for the fence, you will notice the takeoff spot is not long and the horse simply jumps in this style. Rather than defining this as either "loose form" or "reaching," it is most appropriately marked "stylistic reaching." Photographs by Pennington Galleries*

A.

B.

Figs. 2-12A, B—Horses carrying their legs very close together (A) or very far apart (B) in the air should receive slight penalties for their jumping styles, which vary from the ideal pictured in Fig. 2-1B. Photographs by Pennington Galleries

A.

B.

C.

Figs. 2-13A, B, C—Compare the round back of this athletic horse (A) with the flat back (B) and hollow back (C) of the other two animals. In pinning, the flat-backed horse should place above the hollow-backed animal. Photograph A by Budd Studio/B and C by Pennington Galleries

the other hand, the flatbacked horse shows a lack of scope and, even though it may look fairly nice with its legs tucked neatly in front of its chest at a 3-foot 6-inch obstacle, it will never be a "big-time" horse.

Although there may be some truth to this observation, as a judge you must consider the performance the horse actually makes, rather than conjecture as to how nice the horse might be in the future over larger fences. All else being equal, the horse that jumps with a rounded back and its knees down should not be pinned above a flat-backed horse that has its legs tightly folded in front of its chest.

In classes in which the fences are extremely small for the horses, the animals will be unable to have a very round appearance in the back and neck and the tight form that should accompany this; over such low jumps, their front legs will almost touch the ground on the far side of the fence while their hind legs are still pushing off on the near side. Out of necessity, you may end up pinning such a class more on the horses' general way of going and the spots they meet at the fences than on form faults. However, in competitions in which the fences are 3 feet 6 inches or higher for horses, the obstacles will be large enough in proportion to the animals (except in the case of an extremely tall horse) that you will be able to consider all the form faults discussed in this book, including how the horses use their backs and necks.

FLIGHT PATH

Ideal Flight Pattern

Sometimes a horse's form—that is, its use of its legs, back, and neck— may be attractive, but the animal commits other errors over the fence by wavering from the ideal flight pattern. The flight pattern of a horse begins as the animal leaves the ground on the near side of the obstacle and ends as the horse's feet touch the ground on the far side (see Figs. 2-2A, B). Ideally, the horse's landing spot and its takeoff spot should be equidistant from the center of the fence. To simplify the explanation, if a horse leaves the ground 6 feet from the center of the fence, it should land on the far side 6 feet from the center of the fence.

In addition, the horse should approach the middle of a fence without wandering off of a straight line, jump the fence without drifting off that line in the air, and land on the same line. On hunter courses, a horse that deviates from this ideal path commits a flight pattern fault. (The exception is usually a handy hunter class, in which the placement of a previous or upcoming fence may require the horse to jump the current fence at an angle or at some place other than the middle of the fence. These classes are now rarely held, however.)

Maintaining a Line

One of the major flight pattern faults is "drifting," in which the horse leaves the ground on the center line, "drifts" in the air either to the right or left, and lands off the center line (Fig. 2-14). Drifting is penalized because it is a lateral evasion of the rider's aids; it can result in injury to the rider if the horse drifts so far across the fence that the rider's leg catches on the standard; and it suggests that the animal is using an unorthodox jumping style in order to deal with an unsoundness, such as a leg or back problem.

Fig. 2-14—The rider is trying to prevent his horse from "drifting in the air" any farther by using an opening rein. You can see that the horse has already moved off the center line of the obstacle. Photograph by Pennington Galleries

Fig. 2-15—When the horse's body is very close to the standard of the fence, the rider's leg can be injured. Jumping a fence off-center should not be seen in hunter classes unless the course is set in a trappy way that requires it, or the footing to the center of the fence is very bad. Photograph by Pennington Galleries

Another fault is the horse jumping on a line that is not in the middle of the obstacle—that is, approaching, jumping, and landing on a straight line that is either left or right of the middle of the fence. This is not nearly as bad as drifting, but it, too, can cause injury to the rider if the horse jumps too close to the standard (Fig. 2-15).

In scoring, a horse that drifts should be penalized considerably more than a horse that jumps left or right of the center but remains on a straight line before, over, and after the fence. A basic precept of mounted equestrian sports is that a horse should be forthright in its work and not attempt to evade the rider's legs by dropping behind or wandering between them. Therefore, the horse that jumps off center, but remains straight, is considerably better than the horse that wanders across the fence, taking advantage of the few seconds in the air to evade the rider's control.

Even Arc

Whenever a horse has an uneven flight pattern, in which it leaves and lands at different distances from the center of the fence, it should be penalized. Some horses will "overjump" their fences, with their landing distance being greater than their departure distance from the center of the obstacle; while others will "cut down" on the far side of the fence, making the landing distance shorter than the distance of their departure from the center of the obstacle.

Overjumping the fence is associated with an anxious horse that uses the period of time the rider releases it in the air to gain momentum. Although the rider may be able to control the horse's pace until takeoff, few riders have the talent to control a horse well in midair; thus, an anxious horse will seize the occasion to take advantage of the rider in the air, will land far from the fence with a great deal of momentum, and, having been able to stretch its neck forward during the rider's release, will keep its neck outstretched, preventing the rider from collecting it from this long, pulling frame. Reflecting anxiety and disobedience in the horse, overjumping is severely penalized.

Cutting down has already been discussed, but it is mentioned here again because it is the opposite of overjumping the fence. In cutting down, the horse lands closer to the fence than it departed the ground before the fence (see Fig. 2-6). Compared to an anxious horse that overjumps fences, a horse that cuts down is preferable, for cutting down signifies lack of scope, but not bad temperament.

Rhythm

Not only should the flight pattern be considered, but also the rhythm the horse displays as it leaves the ground, flies through the air, and lands. "Getting quick off the ground" is characterized by the horse's front feet quickly patting the ground on the takeoff stride, rather than maintaining the same rhythm the horse had as it approached the fence. A horse that gets quick off the ground is usually a high-strung or "hot" horse that makes other errors related to its temperament—such as overjumping the obstacles. Getting quick demonstrates anxiety in the animal and is heavily penalized in keeping with other faults that relate to nervousness in the horse.

In contrast, "dwelling off the ground" (that is, at takeoff) and "dwelling in the air" are associated with horses of dull, lazy temperament. When a horse dwells off the ground, its jumping ability is hindered by the lack of momentum before it leaves the ground, and the horse's flight and landing may be dangerous. In contrast, a horse that dwells in the air already has completed the crucial takeoff thrust and generally will have enough momentum to make a safe (though not necessarily attractive) landing. For this reason, dwelling in the air is preferable to dwelling off the ground. In comparing these faults associated with dullness to faults associated with nervousness, the faults indicating anxiety are worse because an anxious horse is a greater threat to the rider's safety than is a lazy animal.

PACE AND IMPULSION

Definitions

In simplest terms, *pace* equals speed, and *impulsion* equals thrust. They go hand in hand to a certain degree because as a horse increases its pace, its thrust also increases, both on the flat, as the animal pushes off the ground harder to achieve greater speed, and over fences, when the greater pace allows the horse to launch its body weight more easily. However, there is a point at which a horse needs more impulsion, but not more pace, in order to turn in a first-rate performance—that is, simply going faster will not improve the quality of the round, but having more impulsion will.

For instance, in courses involving tight turns, such as a handy hunter course, a horse cannot create sufficient thrust off the ground at the fences by simply going faster, for the acuteness of the turns restricts the pace. However, a rider can create more impulsion in the horse by adding leg and balancing the horse with hand so that the horse's engine—its hindquarters—will push harder while the rider's hands will restrict the horse from gaining speed. (See Chapter 4 on Equitation on the Flat and Chapter 5 on Equitation over Fences for a more detailed discussion of the rider's control of the horse's impulsion.)

Pace is related to horizontal motion in the horse, for the horse that is asked to go forward by the rider's legs and is unrestricted by the rider's hands will stretch forward into a longer stride, create a faster speed, and move on a flatter frame. In contrast, impulsion is related to vertical motion, for a horse that is asked to go forward by the rider's legs and is restricted by the rider's hands will have a more vertical motion to its strides; while the rider's legs create more energy, the rider's restricting hands cause that energy to be used in upward, thrusting motion.

The Correct Pace

There is no set speed at which every horse should be going when approaching fences. The pace depends upon many things, such as the size of the fences, the horse's length of stride, and the way the course is set. The best rule in judging pace is, "Use your common sense." Does the horse look as though it is going too fast or too slow? Does the round appear dangerous because of excessive speed, or dull because of too little pace? If the answer to any of these questions is "yes," then the horse's pace is inappropriate for the course.

The Correct Impulsion

Judging proper impulsion is considerably more difficult than judging proper pace. Basically, we can equate impulsion with the horse's athletic ability. Does the animal use its hocks well as it takes each stride so that its hindquarters are well under its body? Does the animal rock back onto its hocks when it jumps, or does it simply "jump off its front end," using as little push power from its hocks as possible? If the horse doesn't have impulsive, athletic strides and good, solid thrust off the ground at each fence, it doesn't have enough impulsion. Although impulsion will not be marked separately on the judge's card, it will come into play when considering "way of going" and will be evident in the markings concerning the horse's jumping form, which inevitably suffers when the animal lacks sufficient impulsion.

BENDING

Since much more time is spent going between fences than actually jumping them, the way a horse travels between the obstacles is extremely important and gains more importance as a deciding factor between horses as the competition gets stiffer. To make a horse look its best on course, the rider must keep the animal straight in its body on straight lines and bent in the direction of travel on bending lines (Figs. 2-16A, B, C).

A.

B.

C.

Figs. 2-16A, B, C—A horse's vision, balance, and length of stride are negatively affected when the animal is not bent in the direction of travel (A). In contrast, this horse is properly bent around the turn, while its rider is well-balanced in the center of her mount (B). The third horse (C) is resisting by "drifting" to the outside of the turn, "popping its shoulder" to the right to the point that its neck becomes overly bent to the left. Generally, a horse will try to drift toward the stable area, in-gate, or other place where a group of horses is congregated. Photographs by Pennington Galleries

In a typical hunter course, the horse will be asked to negotiate two straight outside lines, two straight diagonal lines, and five curving lines, which include the beginning and ending circle (Fig. 2-17). Since a large part of every course is performed on curving lines, a chronically unbent animal will not be successful in top-notch competition.

Balance, Vision, and Impulsion

Besides the fact that the unbent horse produces an unattractive performance, there are a few safety reasons for penalizing the animal. As it negotiates corners with its head cranked to the outside, it carries most of its weight on its inside legs. This means it is traveling off-balance, which can cause serious problems in good footing as well as bad.

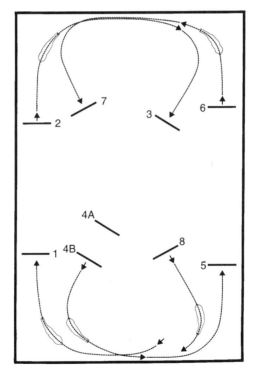

Fig. 2-17—Five bending lines are shown in this diagram of a typical hunter course. Since much of every course is performed on curves, a chronically unbent animal should be heavily penalized. Diagram by the author

When a horse is unbalanced around corners, it has difficulty jumping fences close to them and will sometimes "jump off of one leg." Occasionally, a horse will even run through a fence, because its head is turned so far to the outside that it can't see the obstacle it is galloping toward.

Also associated with the unbent horse is the problem of maintaining enough forward momentum to "make the distances" between the fences. A horse that is not bent around a corner will lose impulsion and shorten its stride by leaning toward the inside of the curve—two faults that make it nearly impossible for the horse to travel to the next fence in the correct number of strides.

As for the aesthetics involved in judging the unbent horse, the combination of a short-strided, unbalanced, and stiff animal is hardly a winning one.

THE NUMBERS

Now to the controversial matter of the "correct number of strides" between fences on a line. In A-rated shows today, the fences are set with a given number of strides intended between them. Each stride may have been figured at 12 feet, or, in major competitions, at 13 feet. The question arises each year, "What about the small-strided horse? Should it be penalized for not making the line in the numbers?" (with "the numbers" meaning the correct number of strides based on the 12-foot or 13-foot stride). The answer is this: if a horse has good form over fences, maintains a suitable pace for the size of the obstacles, and moves well between fences, then it should not be penalized for having added strides.

The problem of riding a course in the numbers is not so great in the hunter division as in the equitation division, for the closer the fences are set, the more crucial it becomes to stick to the designated number of strides. This is not because of the distance between two fences on a line, but because of the distances between these fences and other fences that precede or follow them, since related segments of a course can be drastically affected by the addition of strides. In hunter classes, however, besides negotiating obstacles that have a distance of four strides or less between them, the small horse is not likely to suffer in the quality of its performance from the addition of a single stride. Even for a line of two fences set four strides apart, a small horse can put in an extra stride and look quite nice. The four-stride distance only becomes a problem for a small horse when it is followed by a maximum-length in-and-out. The problem arises when the horse waits to add the fifth stride and has neither the necessary impulsion, nor the long spot, to get through the in-and-out in the designated one or two strides, whichever the case may be.

You should not feel obliged to excuse the erratic performance of a small horse, for it is the rider's responsibility to pick a suitable horse for the competition. If a rider intends to show on the Florida circuit or in the indoor shows in the fall, then he or she must recognize that most big shows are setting the distances based on a 13-foot stride and must keep this in mind when choosing a mount.

Although a horse should not be penalized for adding or deleting strides if those options are appropriate within the framework of a suitable pace and the horse's natural length of stride, you must not excuse faults that result from the horse's size. For example, a small horse may be overfaced by the size of the fences and show its lack of ability at that height by flattening its back in the air or twisting to clear the rails. Similarly, a large horse may not be jumping fences at an appropriate height to demonstrate good form in the air and may be sloppy with its legs, never seeming to reach a peak because its hind legs are still on the ground when the horse is at the zenith of its arc over the fence.

As far as pace is concerned, a large horse usually has an advantage, since it appears relaxed as it casually covers ground. A small horse, on the other hand, often goes beyond appearing brilliant to looking rushed if it attempts the long distances; or, if it tries the other option of adding a stride, it may struggle to jump the fences from a lesser pace.

If a large and a small horse turn in comparable trips, however, you can pin the horses according to your personal taste, for a small, brilliant horse may be more appealing to you than a large, casual horse—or vice versa. As long as the trips are considered equal in every other way, you can pin the one you personally prefer.

CHANGING LEADS

Landing on the Lead; Flying Changes

Many hunter classes are lost by horses that won't go around corners of the ring on the correct lead. I believe the smartest solution for the rider is to teach his horse to land out of the air onto the correct lead at the end of each line by using the outside leg aid while the horse is airborne—the same aid that is used for the basic canter depart. However, both landing on the proper lead and performing a flying change are correct, and a rider is free to use whichever solution he or she prefers.

Counter Canter vs. Cross Canter

As for the horse that lands on the incorrect lead and refuses to perform a flying change, the animal will take one of four options: stay on the counter canter around the entire corner; switch leads in front but not behind, resulting in a cross canter around the entire corner; cross-canter for a few steps before switching completely onto the proper lead; or, cross-canter the corner and switch back onto the counter lead on the approach to the upcoming fence.

Although a horse traveling on the counter canter is not properly balanced on corners, it is preferable for a horse to *remain on the counter lead* than to *maintain a cross canter* through the entire corner, for the cross canter is disjointed in appearance, affects the rider's ability to place the horse properly at the upcoming fence, and causes the horse to be unbalanced. Further considering balance at takeoff, it is preferable for a horse to cross-canter the corner and switch back onto the counter lead just before the fence than to attempt to jump the fence out of the cross canter.

However, in comparing the horse that cross-canters a few steps with the horse that maintains the counter canter around the entire corner, the horse that cross-canters and switches would be preferable, for the animal would be on the proper lead for at least part of the time and would be better balanced for takeoff.

In judging the class, then, the horse that landed on the correct lead after each line and the horse that properly performed the flying changes would be considered equal. However, in top competition, the horse that lands on the correct lead might place higher because its round would look smoother without the interruption of the flying changes. Following the first- and second-place pinning of these two horses, the next would be the horse that cross-cantered a few steps then switched to the proper lead. In fourth place would be the animal that remained on the counter lead around the entire corner and on the approach to the upcoming fence. Fifth place would go to the horse that cross-cantered the corner and switched back to the counter lead on the approach to the fence; and in sixth place would be the horse that cross-cantered the entire corner and jumped the fence out of a cross canter.

Breaking Gait

Besides counter-cantering or cross-cantering the corners, the horse might break gait from a canter into a trot rather than perform a flying change. A break in gait is a serious fault in both classes over fences and on the flat and is worse than a counter canter or cross canter. Breaking gait demonstrates the horse's unwillingness to go forward from the rider's leg and is penalized in accordance with other faults related to lack of forward motion. It would only be pinned above severe behavioral faults, such as refusing at a fence or rearing, and other faults that imply danger to the rider, for instance an extremely fast pace or a knockdown (which is considered worse than a break in gait because of the involvement of the horse's legs with the rails).

Habitual Switching of Leads on Lines

Another error involving leads in the show ring is the switching of leads between fences on a line. This can be a threat to the rider's safety if the switching throws the rider's eye off in finding the proper distance to a fence. Consequently, the horse that habitually switches leads between fences on a line should be heavily penalized.

DISHONEST VS. HONEST HORSE

Dishonest: Unsafe

A "dishonest" horse is one that attempts to evade its rider's commands, and in so doing, threatens the safety of the rider. The worst fault a horse can exhibit in competition is the lack of honesty, for just as this is a major character flaw in a human, so is it in a horse.

Excessive Forward Motion

Although the dishonest horse is usually associated with the lack of forward motion (that is, rearing, refusing to jump a fence, balking at the in-gate or anywhere else in the ring, or attempting to back without having been asked to do so), dishonesty is also associated with horses that use extreme forward motion to frighten or displace the rider. When a horse bolts during a performance—that is, runs away with its rider at some point during the course—it should be heavily penalized, with the severity of the penalty keeping the horse out of the ribbons if at all possible.

Shying, in which the animal quickly moves away from some object in or around the ring, is a mild form of bolting which lasts usually only a second or two and involves sideways, rather than straightforward, movement. Shying can be a minor disobedience or a major one, according to how much the animal has reacted to the object that frightened it and depending on the particular situation.

For instance, a tense horse that persistently shies away from objects in and around the ring should be greatly penalized for not exhibiting the obedience and working attitude we are looking for in a good hunter. However, a horse with a basically good working attitude might shy slightly when an unusual incident occurs, such as a gust of wind blowing down the umbrella over the judge's stand. In this case, the animal is simply surprised, and its reaction is not an indication of its basic attitude toward work. Therefore, the circumstance would call for only a slight penalty, particularly since the animal was subject to a situation that its competitors did not have to deal with when they jumped the course. However, if other faults occur on the course following such an incident—such as the horse speeding up or shying from other objects—then the judge must penalize these faults, for there is only so far one can go in giving the horse the benefit of the doubt.

Lack of Forward Motion

Equally as dangerous as a runaway horse is one that rears, for in both cases, the rider and horse can be seriously injured. Rearing, the ultimate expression of the horse's unwillingness to go forward, should be severely penalized. As in the case of bolting, rearing should keep the competitor out of the ribbons if at all possible, for these disobediences are more potentially dangerous than any other faults the horse can commit.

A refusal at a fence also demonstrates the horse's unwillingness to go forward from the rider's leg, which may present a physical threat to the rider if the horse stops so abruptly that it slings the rider forward into the rails. An honest horse will find some way to help the rider get to the other side of the fence, even from a difficult spot, while a dishonest horse will simply stop on the near side rather than put forth the effort.

Although traditionally the *Rule Book* has considered the penalty for a refusal equal to that for bolting, most judges penalize bolting (running away) more severely because it is commonly believed to be the more dangerous fault of the two. (However, in the extreme case mentioned above in which a refusal results in the fall of a rider, the horse is eliminated from the class.) Also, according to the *Rule Book* prior to 1991, a refusal should have been penalized equally with a knockdown; but in reality, a refusal is penalized more heavily than a knockdown by the majority of judges. The reason is that judges realize an honest horse will attempt to jump a fence, although it may knock it down in doing so, while a dishonest horse will refuse to try to jump the obstacle. Most horsemen appreciate a horse with "heart," that is, a horse that will at least give it a try. In keeping with this attitude, most horsemen hate a "stopper," the horse that won't put forth the effort to try to jump the fence and always looks for a way out.

It is commonly accepted that there is more inherent danger to a rider mounted on an unwilling, dishonest horse than to a rider on a well-intentioned animal that doesn't put forth quite enough effort to clear an obstacle. Therefore, while a horse that has its feet close enough to the fence to bring a rail down presents some threat to the rider's safety, most judges agree that the danger involved in riding a stopper is greater.

Following the 1991 AHSA Convention in Baltimore, MD, the *Rule Book* changed "Article 2426. Faults" from designating specific penalties for a refusal, bolting, and a knockdown. Now the rule lists them along with many other errors and states, "The following faults are scored according to the judge's opinion and, depending on severity, may be considered minor or major faults." This allows judges to use their "horse sense" in penalizing these errors.

Honest But Unsafe

Next, we'll consider the horse that does not intend to harm its rider but nonetheless performs in an unsafe manner. The horse that falls into this category is often the nice horse ridden by an inadequate rider.

Too Fast, Too Slow

When a rider becomes anxious about a class over fences, he or she may charge around the course in an effort to get over the obstacles in "any old way." The result is a horse that approaches the fences with too much pace, making the round appear dangerous.

At the other extreme is the rider who uses too little leg on his horse, resulting in the animal approaching each fence so slowly that it looks as though it will land on a fence before the course is completed. Since both the overly fast and overly slow rounds are incorrect, horses that demonstrate these extremes should be severely penalized, with the round that exhibits excessive speed being penalized more than the round that is excessively slow; for again, danger is the deciding factor, and a rider is less likely to be injured in a round that is too slow than in one that is too fast.

Knockdowns

In good company, a knockdown will keep a horse from being pinned, but occasionally during a show, a judge must pin a horse with a knockdown for lack of enough horses in the class to allow any options. As stated in the *Rule Book* prior to 1991, a knockdown with any part of the horse's body in front of the stifle should be penalized twice as much as a knockdown with any part of the horse's body behind the stifle. This was in keeping with the rule for touches, in which a front touch was penalized twice as much as a hind touch. Although these specific designations were removed in 1991 by the changes in "Article 2426. Faults," most judges still penalize twice as much for front end knockdowns or touches as for the same errors in the hind end.

When you are watching a knockdown, the reason behind the severity of the penalty for this fault may not be obvious, for a horse may roll a rail yet remain in good form and make a safe landing. However, the penalty for the knockdown is based on the show ring's simulation of fences in a hunt field—fences which are usually fixed and could present great danger to the horse and rider if the horse caught its feet on the unyielding obstacle. The catching of front feet on a fence presents a much greater chance of an accident than does involvement of hind feet, since the horse could flip over if its front end became hung in the fence. Even in the show ring, where the fences give way to pressure, a horse can become entangled in the rails during flight and on landing and have an accident. Therefore, given the show ring's simulation of hunting obstacles and the possibility of an accident occurring even when the rails give way, the penalty for a knockdown is deservedly severe.

Summary

As noted, some basic characteristics of a dishonest horse are: bolting, rearing, refusing to jump, balking at the in-gate, or backing up without having been given the command to do so. In contrast, an honest, but unsafe horse will commit faults such as: going around the course excessively fast, due to an anxious rider; going excessively slow, due to a passive rider; or knocking down a rail, which judges usually consider preferable to a refusal because it shows the horse to be one that is honest in its intentions, rather than a dishonest "quitter."

As a general rule, a horse that shows honesty in its approach to jumping a course of fences should place above a horse that has dishonest characteristics, for a rider is safer on a horse that tries to please him than on one that attempts to thwart his commands.

3

CONFORMATION CLASSES

GENERAL OBSERVATIONS

In judging conformation classes, you are considering the horse's physical makeup as it relates to both performance and soundness. Since much of the available information on this topic has been written by veterinarians who deal daily with the negative results of poor conformation, you should not only use your firsthand experience as a horseman, but also make an effort to read veterinary books and journals in order to be competent to judge these classes.

Before we delve into the specifics of judging horses on the line, let's establish some generalities. First and foremost, a judge should consider a horse's *structural composition*—that is, its body proportions and joint angles—since a horse that is well-proportioned and has the proper angles will have the greatest chance of being sound, balanced, and athletic. Problems of proportion—such as a short neck, long back, or small hindquarters—are heavily penalized. So, too, are angular problems—such as a steep shoulder, a hip or hind leg that is too straight, sickle hocks, or pasterns that are overly upright, to name a few.

Your second consideration is *physical defects*—malformations, resulting from poor structural composition or from injury, that have the potential for producing lameness. Those that appear to be a result of poor structural composition are more heavily penalized than those that are apparently a result of injury. The reason for this is that a horse with a defect related to poor structural composition will continually put stress on the affected area, making recovery difficult, if not impossible. On the other hand, a horse that has a defect as a result of an injury that was not related to poor conformation will only have the severity of the injury itself to contend with during recovery, without additional conformational stress.

Thirdly, we need to distinguish *defects*—such as a splint, capped elbow, bucked shin, capped hock, curb, bog spavin, bowed tendon, bone spavin, thoroughpin, sidebone, osselets, and ringbone—from *blemishes*, which are malformations that do not cause unsoundness. Such things as windpuffs, a cupped indentation in a horse's neck, and superficial scars are blemishes and are the least penalized of conformation faults because they are not a hindrance to the horse's quality of performance or serviceability.

Finally, consider the horse's *soundness*. According to the *AHSA Rule Book*, "Unless specific division rules state otherwise, all animals except stallions and mares in breeding classes must be serviceably sound for horse show purposes—i.e., such animal must not show evidence of lameness, broken wind or complete loss of sight in either eye."

Although most people can detect a horse that limps and understand the necessity of penalizing this unsoundness, few people are knowledgeable concerning "broken wind." In its old interpretation, *broken wind* was synonymous with the term *heavy*. Heavy means that the horse has grown fibrous tissue in the air spaces of its lungs that makes it difficult for the animal to exhale. When a horse is heavy, it uses the following internal sequence to force the air out of its body: it abruptly lifts the abdominal muscles, which push the intestines forward, pressing the diaphragm into the lungs and forcing the air out. Since the heavy condition affects the horse's ability to exhale, the animal retains too much carbon dioxide and can't get enough air out to allow a sufficient amount of fresh air to come in. Therefore, a heavy horse will pant in an effort to catch its breath and will display dilated nostrils, as well as the violent upward abdominal motions. On a "good day," which is usually cool and clear, a heavy horse may be able to jump a course of eight fences without having severe problems; however, in a hot, dusty environment, the horse can be in distress after two or three fences. Since competition in an arena is intended to showcase horses capable of carrying a rider hunting, if you are able to detect a heavey horse while it is jogging in a conformation class, the animal must be disqualified from placing because it is serviceably unsound.

A heavey condition is not the only cause of respiratory sounds on exhalation, for on occasion you will hear a horse making noise as it exhales with "false nostrils." The false nostril (or "alar fold") is an extra flap of skin between the outer nostril and the passageway through which the horse breathes. (You can see part of the false nostril as you stand facing the animal, and if you run your finger between the outer and inner nostril, you will find that the two join only a few inches from the opening to the nose.) A horse that makes noise with this flap has learned that it can control the muscles to the nose and does so only on occasion as a habit, rather than on a regular basis as a result of a physical defect. You can detect this fault as a vibration in the nostrils as the horse makes a blowing sound through its nose. It is a fault akin to ringing the tail or pinning the ears in that it represents a horse's lack of relaxation, willingness, and concentration on its work. As an indication of a less than desirable attitude, "false nostrils" is slightly penalized; but it should not be considered an unsoundness.

Another noticeable breathing sound is "roaring," which can be detected during inhalation. The rattling breathing of a roarer is caused by paralysis of the airway in the horse's head. The constriction occurs where the airway passes through the back of the animal's mouth, before it reaches the trachea. A roarer makes a whistling sound during inhalation and a fluttering sound during exhalation as the air crosses the animal's vocal cords. As long as the horse does not have to exert itself too much, the roaring condition may not severely hinder its performance. For instance, a roarer might be able to go around three courses of eight fences back-to-back and not be in distress, while a heavey horse usually cannot exert itself that long without having severe problems. However, both the roarer and the heavey horse would be in trouble in the hunt field. Although the heavey condition is worse than roaring, both are unsoundnesses affecting stamina and must be penalized equally by denying the horse a ribbon. Thus, when the term "broken wind" is used in the *Rule Book*, it not only encompasses the older meaning of "heavey," but also the respiratory unsoundness known as "roaring."

Since we will be dealing with many specifics throughout this chapter, it is important to keep in mind these general observations:

1. Good proportions and proper joint angles (that is, the animal's structural composition) are the most important features of a conformation horse. Therefore, good proportions and angles accompanied by a mild defect or blemish should pin above poor proportions and angles with no defects or blemishes.

2. Defects that are related to poor structural composition should be more heavily penalized than those that are solely a result of injury; and because defects have the potential to cause unsoundness, they should be more heavily penalized than blemishes, which do not affect soundness.

3. Unsoundness of a horse's legs; respiratory unsoundness (except for "false nostrils"); or blindness must prevent a horse from being pinned.

Throughout this chapter, mention will be made of structural faults and injury as they relate to specific defects in the horse. Although poor nutrition is a third cause of abnormalities in the horse, I have chosen not to discuss nutrition as it relates to defects, since the vast majority of trainers who enter animals in conformation classes have sufficient knowledge of equine nutrition to provide for the basic dietary needs of their animals. For the most part, then, defects in the conformation horse will be a result of injury or structural predisposition rather than nutritional deficiency.

In order to present the following information in such a way that the reader can appreciate the relative penalties for the faults, I have listed comparative defects in order of severity—ranging from most to least serious—as often as possible. Although these comparisons give a general guide for judging, when in the show ring you must take into consideration the degree of severity of the defects on the specific horses being judged and pin accordingly.

A Comparative Guide to Judging Defects
(from most to least serious)

1. ringbone (most serious)	7. bog spavin
2. osselets	8. curb
3. sidebone	9. splint
4. bone spavin	10. capped hock
5. thoroughpin	11. capped elbow
6. bowed tendon	12. bucked shins (least serious)

These comparisons have been determined considering the worst possible effects of each of these defects (that is, the degree of unsoundness that each can cause at its worst and the horse's chance of recovery), and the degree of severity that could be present and still render the horse sound for jogging. These comparisons are also limited to the outward perception of the flaw, since a judge does not have access to x rays.

A SYSTEM FOR JUDGING CONFORMATION

Side View, Near Side

As stated in the *AHSA Rule Book*, the criteria for judging a conformation class are "quality, substance and soundness." Begin judging a strip class by standing far enough away from the side of the first horse in line that you can form a general opinion of the animal's proportions and angles. Since it is easy to overlook conformation faults unless you have a system of examination, you may want to use the procedure outlined here, beginning with a side view on the near side of the animal.

Start at the poll of the horse and run your glance along the animal's topline—that is, the crest, withers, back, and croup to the dock—to see if the topline is smooth (Fig. 3-1). The crest should be slightly arched and athletic-looking. If it is unusually muscular and studdish, it is penalized more than if it is flat and weak, since an overly muscular neck is less yielding and flexible than a flat neck, and contributes less to the animal's bending, flexion, and balance. The withers should fit smoothly into the topline, and the top of the shoulder should blend into the withers. Any excess protrusion of bone from the shoulder or withers is penalized.

The animal's back, from the middle of the withers to the area in the loins just above the point of the hip, should be approximately one-third the length of the horse's body from chest to hindquarters (see Fig. 3-5). An overly long back is penalized for the weakness it indicates. The croup should be curved, not pointed; the hip should blend smoothly into the loins and croup; and the horse's tail should fit naturally into the topline and sit high, rather than drooping off the horse's rump.

After examining the topline, consider the horse's depth of body in the chest, barrel, and flank, and notice any malformation of the horse's frame that would diminish this space in which the internal organs lie. Throughout the body, the animal should appear rounded or "filled out." This

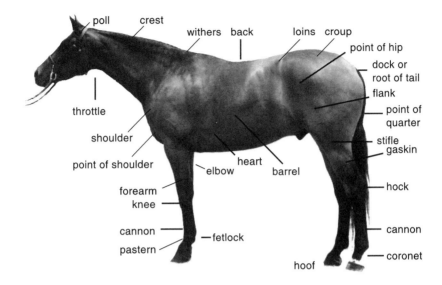

Fig. 3-1—This is an excellent example of a top quality conformation horse, with the basic body parts labeled for reference. Photograph by Budd Studio

doesn't mean the horse should look obese, as though it isn't in work; but if the animal is thin, with its shoulders, ribs, and hips poking out and the flesh sinking in around them, then penalize it. (Actually, the person responsible for the care of the horse ought to be penalized!)

Now that you have examined the topline and depth of body, look at the horse's head. The animal's head should fit the body, rather than being abnormally large or small. The throttle should be well-defined and smoothly connect the head to the neck. The neck must be of a sufficient length and arc to provide the horse with a means of balance while jumping; both a short neck and a ewe neck (commonly called an "upside-down neck") are heavily penalized, for they restrict the horse's ability to keep its balance and thus they affect the animal's athletic ability as a whole (Fig. 3-2). A short neck is penalized more than a ewe neck because, unsightly as a ewe neck is, if it is long it contributes more to bending and balance than does a short neck.

The horse's shoulder must be long and sloping. A shoulder that is too steep and short is heavily penalized because it restricts the horse's length

Fig. 3-2—A ewe neck, being muscular along the underside instead of at the crest, gives the lower part of the neck a convex appearance. Illustration adapted from a sketch by the author

of stride and smoothness of gaits. A line from the middle of the withers to the point of the shoulder and down to the elbow should form approximately a 90-degree angle (Figs. 3-3, 3-4).

The angle of the hip must be sufficiently acute to keep the hind leg from falling too straight from the stifle joint. The connection of the ilium and femur should be at approximately a 90-degree angle (Figs. 3-3, 3-4). The horse's haunches must not appear hiked up or dropped down from the animal's front portion; the croup should be approximately the same height as the withers (Fig. 3-5). (In young horses, the haunches will sometimes grow sooner than the withers, and as the horse matures, the

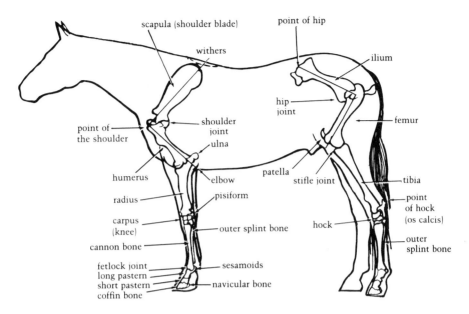

Fig. 3-3—*The proper shoulder and hip angles of this horse allow freedom of movement and prevent excess weight from being placed directly on the animal's limbs. Illustration adapted from a sketch by the author*

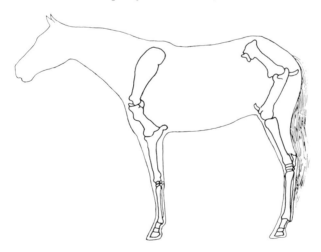

Fig. 3-4—*Compare the steep shoulder and hip angles in this drawing to the correct angles shown in Fig. 3-3. You can see that more pressure is placed downward on the limbs when the angles are too wide. Notice also how the change of the angles has affected the horse's silhouette. Illustration adapted from a sketch by the author*

forehand will grow to match the haunches. Although you would make note of the tall haunches in a class of young horses, you should not penalize it as severely as you would when judging an older animal.)

From this side perspective, notice the horse's stance. When properly positioned by its handler, a horse stands with its legs square in front and with at least one hind leg placed with the point of the hock and back of the fetlock on an imaginary line that extends straight from the point of the quarter to the ground (Fig. 3-5).

If an animal stands with its front or hind feet too far under or with its feet camped in front or behind, it should be penalized (Figs. 3-6A, B). Standing under in front is more heavily penalized than camping in front because standing under overloads the forelimbs, causing excessive wear to the bones and fatigue of the ligaments and tendons, and predisposes the horse to falling, while camping in front may indicate a soundness problem, such as navicular, but does not present a safety problem.

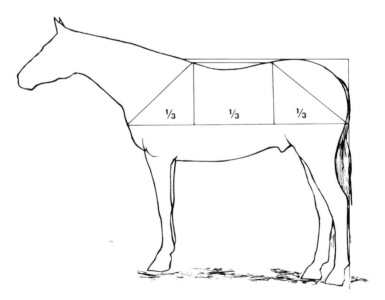

Fig. 3-5—*This horse's croup is the same height as its withers, and the animal is standing properly positioned so that its correct conformation is evident in the direct line through the point of the quarter, the point of the hock, and the back of the fetlock. The trapezoid shows the length of the horse's back to be correctly one-third the length of the horse's body. Illustration adapted from a sketch by the author*

When a horse stands too far under behind, you should look for the structural fault "sickle hocks" and related defects—bone spavin, curb, and cow hocks. (Sickle hocks, bone spavin, curb, and cow hocks will be discussed in the sections Side View, Hind Leg (Near Side), and Rear View.)

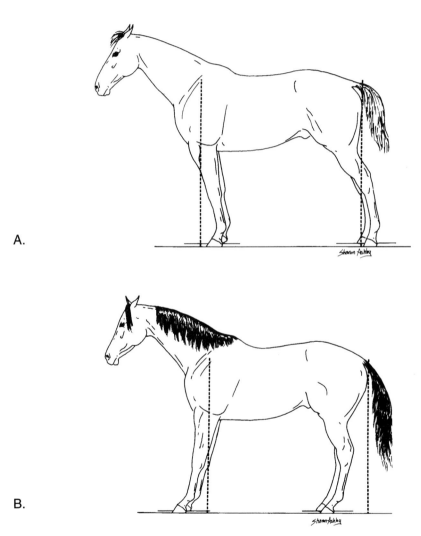

A.

B.

Figs. 3-6A, B—The drawings show a horse standing under in front and camped behind (A), and another standing camped in front and under behind (B). Drawings by Sharon Ashby

If the animal stands camped out behind, look for upright pasterns that might be the cause. Since a hunter must engage its hocks to jump safely, a horse that stands under behind, with its hocks too far underneath its body, is preferable to one that camps behind, with its hocks built back of its body.

Side View, Front Leg (Near Side)

Move closer to the horse to visually examine its legs. Starting with the near front leg, examine the animal from foot to elbow. Check the hoof to see if it is in proportion to the size of the animal and if it properly connects with the leg on the same angle as the pastern (Fig. 3-7). Although a horse that has foundered will not likely enter a conformation class, you should notice any ripples or "rings" on the hooves that would indicate this problem (Fig. 3-8). Since the rings are only an outward indication of some type of internal turmoil and cause no unsoundness themselves, they should be slightly penalized. (The sign that would confirm founder is the dropped sole of the foot. However, since you must not pick up the hoof during this examination, you therefore cannot penalize for the dropped sole, since it may or may not accompany the rings.)

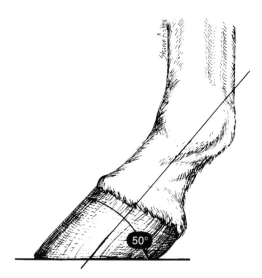

Fig. 3-7—This front foot and pastern are correctly angled at 50 degrees. Drawing by Sharon Ashby

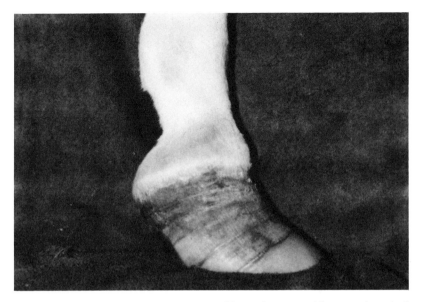

Fig. 3-8—Founder rings are very noticeable on this animal because their dark color is contrasted against a white hoof. On a horse with a dark hoof, the same growth pattern and rippled appearance would suggest founder, but the dark coloration of the blood seen through the hoof wall would not be so obvious, if it were apparent at all. Photograph by Sheila Ellison

In the area of the coronary band and just above, check for signs of sidebone, low ringbone, and high ringbone. Sidebone—a hardening of the cartilages of the foot into bone, caused by concussion—can be found on the outside, inside, or both sides of the foot just above the heels (Fig. 3-9). Although sidebone often develops as part of the natural aging process, a horse that has this condition is heavily penalized because: (1) the animal no longer has the cartilage cushion necessary to minimize trauma from jumping; (2) the bone formation can cause mechanical interference to the foot action; and (3) acting as bone, rather than as a cushion, the formation can fracture.

The defects "low ringbone" and "high ringbone" are so named because of their location on the horse's leg. Low ringbone—a bulging ring around the coronet—affects the coffin joint. High ringbone—a bulging ring approximately 1 inch above the coronet—affects the pastern joint, which, of course, is higher up the horse's leg (Figs. 3-10A, B). (Although

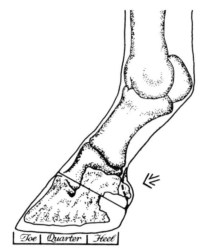

Fig. 3-9—Sidebone may be detected visually in the area just above the horse's heel and can be found on either side or both sides of the foot. The dotted line shows a horse's normal shape in this area, while the solid line indicates the bulge of sidebone. Illustration adapted from a drawing by Sharon Ashby

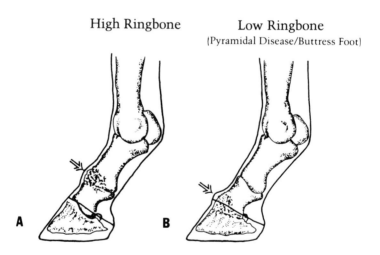

Figs. 3-10A, B—High ringbone occurs in the pastern joint and can be seen approximately 1 inch above the coronet (A), while low ringbone (known also as pyramidal disease or "buttress foot") affects the coffin joint and is found at the coronet (B). Illustration adapted from a drawing by Sharon Ashby

"low ringbone" and "sidebone" are found in the area of the coronary band, low ringbone is differentiated visually as a formation that circles the entire coronary band, while sidebone is seen only on the sides of the foot, at the portion of the coronary band above the heels.) Both low and high ringbone can lead to degenerative arthritis in the involved joint, or can cause the joining of the bones on each side of the joint into a single piece. Ringbone, whether high or low, should be penalized more heavily than sidebone.

Observe the slope of the horse's pastern, which should match the angle of the hoof. (The ideal pastern and hoof angle is about 50 degrees in the front legs and slightly more upright in the hind legs. The difference between front and hind angulation should not be greater than 5 degrees.) If a horse has an overly upright pastern, the result will be a shorter, less athletic stride and excess concussion to the bones in the leg and foot (Figs. 3-11A, B). In contrast, an overly sloping pastern will produce a longer stride, but it will be weak and cause excess pressure to be placed on the heel and the soft-tissue supporting structures in the back of the leg (Figs. 3-12A, B). In scoring, penalize the upright pastern more heavily than the overly sloping pastern because of the limiting effect the steep pastern has on the horse's length of stride.

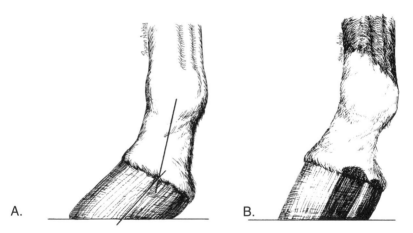

A.   B.

Figs. 3-11A, B—When the foot axis is not the same as the pastern axis, the difference in angulation is called a "broken foot." Notice in the first drawing that the pastern is extremely steep (A). When both the foot axis and pastern axis are excessively steep, the horse is said to have a "club foot." Drawings by Sharon Ashby

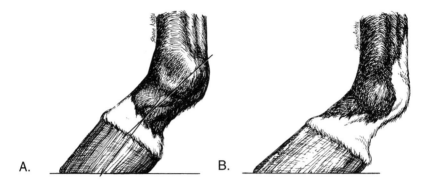

A.   B.

Figs. 3-12A, B—In this "broken foot," the hoof is on a proper axis and the pastern is too sloping, a formation known as a "coon foot" (A). When both the foot and pastern angles are too closed, the horse has a "sloping foot" (B). Drawings by Sharon Ashby

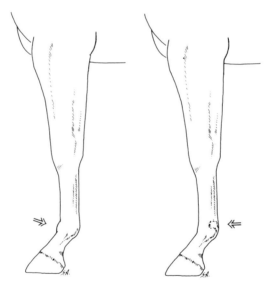

Fig. 3-13 (left)—Osselets appear as a bulge on the front of the fetlock and usually extend at least halfway around the joint. Illustration adapted from a drawing by Sharon Ashby

Fig. 3-14 (right)—Found on the side of the fetlock joint, a windpuff is a blemish seen in many hardworking horses. Since it does not cause lameness, it should only be mildly penalized. Illustration adapted from a drawing by Sharon Ashby

Move your eyes to the area of the fetlock and examine the horse for osselets and windpuffs. Osselets appear as a bulge on the front of the fetlock, extending at least halfway around the joint in most cases (Fig. 3-13). The bulge under the skin is caused by a deposit of calcium, formed as a result of trauma that produced arthritis in the fetlock joint and inflammation of the joint capsule. A horse with osselets should be pinned above an animal with ringbone and below a horse with sidebone—although we hope that no horse in the class will have any of these serious faults!

A windpuff, which is a swelling on the side of the fetlock joint, is found either on the inside or on the outside of the front (or hind) legs (Fig. 3-14). It is seen in many hardworking horses and does not cause lameness. Being a blemish, a windpuff is penalized only in the mildest degree.

Moving up the leg to the cannon bone, look for a bucked shin, which is a swelling on the front of the cannon bone generally caused by concussion and related to speed and fatigue (Fig. 3-15). Bucked shins usually are found in the forelimbs, rather than hind limbs, and the condition

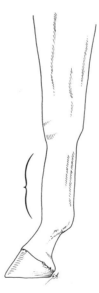

Fig. 3-15—Bucked shins are penalized mildly, for although the blemish left after the horse has returned to soundness may be unsightly, it does not present a problem of recurrent unsoundness. Drawing by Sharon Ashby

generally occurs in both forelegs at the same time (although this is a defect mainly found in race horses and rarely seen in hunters, unless they came from the track). If a bucked shin is present in only one limb, direct trauma to the area is most likely the cause.

Since a horse with bucked shins can have complete recovery if rested for a proper length of time, this defect is not considered a serious fault. "Complete recovery" means a return to soundness without recurring problems, although the swelling on the front of the cannon bone may remain as a blemish. In judging, you should penalize bucked shins less than you would penalize: a capped elbow, which can be continually aggravated (bucked shins are generally nonrecurrent); a capped hock, in which the tendon may be damaged and flexion reduced; and splints, which may grow and impinge on tendons and ligaments. Bucked shins are penalized less than any of the other defects mentioned in this chapter, for although the blemish left after the horse has returned to soundness may be unsightly, it does not present a soundness problem.

In the area between the fetlock and knee, look for splints. A splint is a bony growth usually found about 3 inches below a horse's knee on the inside of a front leg, but it may be found at other locations on both the inside and outside of the legs along the splint bones (see Fig. 3-34A, B). Caused by hard training, interference (or another type of blow to the leg), or poor conformation, splints most often appear in the forelegs. They frequently develop from hard work that causes a disturbance in the ligament between the inside or the outside splint bone and the cannon bone, which results in new bone growth. When seen in a conformation class, a splint should not be considered a serious defect unless it is related to poor structure or is located toward the back of a splint bone so that it is obviously impinging upon a tendon or ligament. Although you look for splints on the outside of the near foreleg at this point in the examination, you'll usually be able to see both inside and outside splints more clearly when viewing the horse from the front.

A bowed tendon—another of the serious defects not likely to be found in a conformation class—appears in the area between the fetlock and knee (Fig. 3-16A, B, C, D). A bowed tendon is caused by severe strain to the tendon sheath, which results in development of scar tissue. Although the condition can be present in the hind limbs, it is generally an injury of the forelegs and is most often seen in horses with overly sloping pasterns. With a chronic problem, the horse may be sound walking and trotting, but will go lame in hard work. When judging the bowed

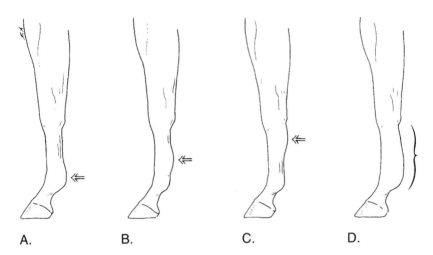

A.   B.   C.   D.

Figs. 3-16A, B, C, D—Found between the fetlock and knee, a bowed tendon is classified as low (A), middle (B), or high (C), or it may involve all three areas (D). Drawings by Sharon Ashby

tendon, consider it to be worse than a bucked shin, capped elbow, capped hock, splint, curb, or bog spavin, but preferable to thoroughpin, bone spavin, sidebone, osselets, and ringbone.

Just below the knee, check for the horse being "cut out under the knee" or "tied in behind the knee." Both of these conditions are structural weaknesses that cause the tendons behind the leg to be pulled around a curve within the knee by the muscles above. This action, similar to a rope running through a pulley, prevents a straight line of force as the horse places the foot during motion. Since "cut out under the knee" and "tied in behind the knee" have the same negative effect, they receive equal penalty (Figs. 3-17A, B).

If the knee is set too far back ("calf knee") or if it hangs over the front of the cannon bone ("bucked knee" or "over in the knee"), penalize the horse, since these structural faults cause weight to be distributed improperly down the leg and can lead to unsoundness (Figs. 3-18A, B). Calf knees are more severely penalized than bucked knees, because they are more likely to lead to unsoundness during hard work. Comparing these faults to those above, calf knees and bucked knees are worse than legs being tied in below the knees or cut out under the knees.

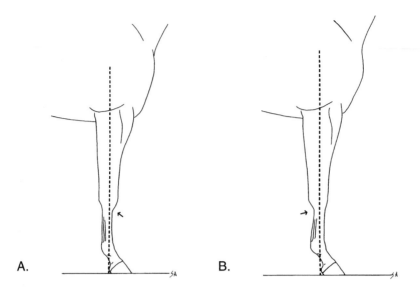

Figs. 3-17A, B—*"Cut out under the knee" (A), and "tied in behind the knee" (B). Drawings by Sharon Ashby*

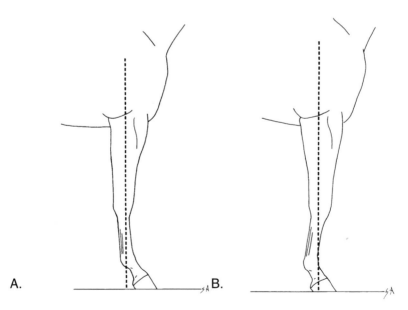

Figs. 3-18A, B—*"Calf knee" (A), and "bucked knee" or "over in the knee" (B). Drawings by Sharon Ashby*

Look for a bulging contour of the knee that suggests "degenerative joint disease," commonly referred to as DJD or "carpitis" (Fig. 3-19). If a horse's knee is unusually shaped when compared to a normal knee on the other leg, suspect DJD. Although you cannot determine the extent of DJD without using x rays, you must heavily penalize any indication of this defect, for it is a progressive disease that is worse than any of the other knee abnormalities discussed in this chapter.

After examining the knee, consider the horse's forearm and the manner in which the leg attaches to the body. The forearm should be well-developed, with more emphasis being placed on this quality in mature horses than in young ones. As for the attachment of the leg to the body, the leg should extend straight down from the joint so that the horse's weight is equally distributed between the front and back of the leg (Fig. 3-20).

Look in the area of the elbow for any swelling of a "capped elbow" (also called "shoe boil"), which is bursitis in the elbow usually caused by

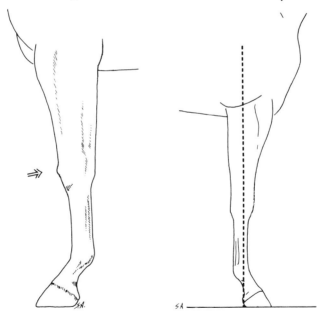

Fig. 3-19 (left)—Degenerative joint disease (DJD or "carpitis"). Illustration adapted from a drawing by Sharon Ashby

Fig. 3-20 (right)—A horse's foreleg should extend straight down from the joint, as in this example. Drawing by Sharon Ashby

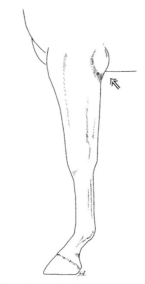

Fig. 3-21—"Capped elbow" or "shoe boil." Drawing by Sharon Ashby

the shoe on the foot of the affected limb hitting the elbow while the horse is lying down (Fig. 3-21). A "capped elbow" is not heavily penalized in comparison with most of the defects in this chapter (see A Comparative Guide to Judging Defects, pg. 61), since it is due to injury rather than a structural fault in the horse.

Having examined the outside of the left foreleg, begin the same process on the inside of the right foreleg by standing across from the horse's barrel on the near side, so you can see the inside of the right foreleg on an oblique angle. Once again, start with the foot and work up, looking for the above-mentioned faults and penalizing those you find.

Side View, Hind Leg (Near Side)

Once you have finished looking at the inside of the right foreleg, move toward the back of the horse so you can view the left hind leg from a side perspective. Many of the desirable features of a front foot should be present in a hind foot: the foot being the proper size for the horse's body and on the same angle as the pastern; the foot being neither overly steep, nor overly sloping; and the hoof wall being smooth, showing no signs of founder rings. Moving upward to the coronary band, where sidebone and ringbone can be found in the forelegs, look for any abnormalities, although the incidence of these particular defects in the hind legs is rare.

The slope of the hind foot and pastern should differ slightly from that of the forefoot and pastern. While the slope of a front foot should be about 50 degrees, the hind foot should be slightly more upright (Fig. 3-22). As stated earlier, the difference between front and hind angulation must not exceed 5 degrees. In scoring the hind legs—just as in scoring the front—penalize pasterns that are excessively upright more than those that are too sloping.

Although osselets are not common in the hind legs, windpuffs are found frequently in both the front and hind legs in the fetlock area. Again, windpuffs do not produce lameness and should be mildly penalized.

Splints and bowed tendons, found in the area of the cannon bone on the front legs, are rarely seen in the hind legs. Directly above the cannon bone, however, is the hock area, in which many problems can develop.

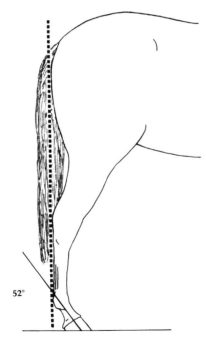

Fig. 3-22—The slope of the hind foot and pastern should be slightly more upright than 50 degrees. The difference between angulation of the front and hind limbs should not exceed 5 degrees. Illustration adapted from a sketch by the author

A "sickle hock" is a structural fault characterized by the angle of the hock joint being so acute (when viewed from the side) that the horse is standing under from the hock down (Fig. 3-23). A sickle hock is often responsible for the development of bone spavin and curb and is a very undesirable feature in the hind limbs.

In a "straight hind leg," the hock joint is so erect (when viewed from the side) that it causes excess concussion to the leg (Fig. 3-24). This structural fault can cause bog spavin (a swelling of the hock joint capsule from trauma) and upward fixation of the patella (a condition in which the horse's hind leg is locked in extension, or, in milder cases, the hind leg "catches" as the horse moves). Comparing a "straight hind leg" to a "sickle hock," the horse with the sickle hock should be more heavily penalized.

Besides these structural faults, there are also a number of defects that may appear in the hock area. At the front of the hock, look for bog spavin, which, as mentioned earlier, is a swelling of the hock joint capsule

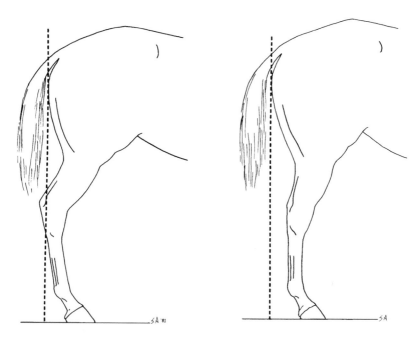

Fig. 3-23 (left)—Sickle hock. Drawing by Sharon Ashby

Fig. 3-24 (right)—Straight hind leg. Drawing by Sharon Ashby

usually caused by trauma (Fig. 3-25). Bog spavin may result from trauma associated with conformation—as in the case of a horse that is too straight in the hock—or from trauma brought on by jumping a horse while it is too young, jumping too often, or stopping or turning a horse quickly. In some cases, bog spavin has two accompanying swellings, one on the outside of the leg and one on the inside. These swellings are sometimes confused with thoroughpin, which actually occurs higher in the hock area.

"Thoroughpin" is a more serious defect than bog spavin, for although bog spavin can cause lameness due to the irritation within the joint, thoroughpin is a progressive condition in which adhesions form around a tendon in the hock, which finally results in complete loss of the gliding capability of the tendon within its sheath. Thoroughpin can be found just in front of the point of the hock at a level slightly higher than the point where secondary bog spavin swellings occur (Fig. 3-26).

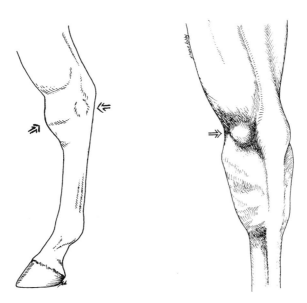

Fig. 3-25 (left)—The arrow on the left indicates the position and swelling of bog spavin. The arrow on the right points to a secondary bog swelling. Compare the position of secondary bog spavin to the position of thoroughpin in Fig. 3-26 (right). Illustration adapted from a drawing by Sharon Ashby

Fig. 3-26 (right)—Thoroughpin. Drawing by Sharon Ashby

On the point of the hock, look for a "capped hock," the least serious of all hock faults that will be mentioned. A capped hock is bursitis caused by trauma to the point of the hock and is usually incurred through the horse kicking a wall or the tailgate of a trailer (Fig. 3-27). The condition is characterized by a swelling at the point of the hock and may be accompanied by curb (discussed below). A capped hock is preferable to the other hock faults because, although it can be a defect (that is, can cause unsoundness, particularly if the horse continually reinjures the hock), it is usually only a blemish (that is, the swelling remains visible, but does not cause unsoundness, after the inflammation has subsided).

Just below the point of the hock, look for signs of a "curb"—an inflammation of one of the ligaments in the hock, usually caused by extreme exertion or by trauma from kicking stable or trailer walls (Fig. 3-28). On a horse with sickle hocks or cow hocks, however, curb is often a result of poor structure. In judging, penalize a curb more heavily than a capped hock, but less than a bog spavin, thoroughpin, or bone spavin (discussed below).

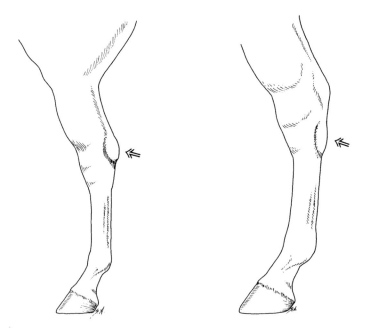

Fig. 3-27 (left)—Capped hock. Drawing by Sharon Ashby

Fig. 3-28 (right)—Curb. Drawing by Sharon Ashby

After considering the major hock problems best detected from a side view, look at the horse's gaskin to see whether or not it is well developed and at the proper angle (see Figs. 3-1, 3-3, 3-4). If the gaskin is too steep, it should be penalized for causing excess pressure to be exerted directly down on the hind leg.

Once examination of the left hind leg is complete, step back into place next to the horse's barrel where, from an oblique viewpoint, you can begin the same process with the off hind leg, starting with the foot and working up. All of the aforementioned faults which can be seen from this vantage point should be penalized.

In addition, look for "bone spavin" on the inside of each hind leg on the lower part of the hock (Figs. 3-29, 3-30). A "bone spavin," frequently called a "jack spavin" or "jack," begins with inflammation of the covering of the bone or of the bony tissue itself. The inflammation is usually caused by trauma associated with jumping a horse while it is too young, jumping too often, or stopping a horse quickly, or by trauma related to poor conformation such as sickle hocks, cow hocks, or thin hocks. The

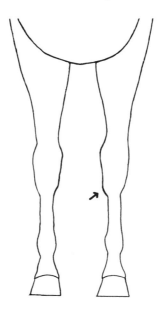

Fig. 3-29—*In this view of the horse's hind legs from a front perspective, notice the difference in the shape of the normal hock on the left and the hock on the right with bone spavin (indicated by arrow). Illustration adapted from a sketch by the author*

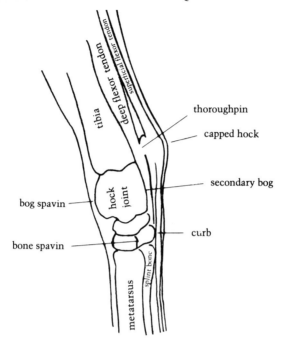

Fig. 3-30—The locations of conformation faults in and around the hock, as viewed on the inside of the right hind leg. Illustration adapted from a sketch by the author

inflammation results in new bone growth that, in some cases, merges the lower two joints of the hock on the inside of the hind leg. The horse will generally become lame during the bone growth process involving these joints, but may return to soundness once the merger of these joints is complete. However, the percentage of horses whose joints fuse, allowing them to become sound again, is not very high. In comparative scoring, bone spavin is penalized more heavily than any of the other hock defects (thoroughpin, bog spavin, curb, and capped hock) because if the involved joints do not fuse, the horse may become permanently lame.

Front View

While you are walking from the side to the front of the horse, notice the animal's general expression and attitude. Ideally, a horse should have wide-set, intelligent-looking eyes that have a kind expression. An eye that is cloudy, indicating complete loss of sight, should eliminate the horse from receiving a ribbon.

While an animal is being shown on the line, it should be relaxed enough to stand still, but appear attentive, "wearing its ears well" by carrying them pointed forward rather than "pinning the ears" back, which is an indication of a bad attitude. Long, floppy ears are mildly penalized because they detract from the overall picture of elegance that an ideal strip horse should have.

Stand in front of the animal on an imaginary center line that bisects the horse (generally, you can see past the person showing the animal, but if not, ask him or her to move slightly to one side so you can get a good view). Consider the breadth of the horse in proportion to the depth of its body, making sure the chest is sufficiently wide, as well as deep, to give plenty of room for the heart and lungs. A well-formed chest should have an upside-down V shape that indicates proper musculature in the attachments of the front legs to the body and of the neck to the chest (Fig. 3-31).

Next, look at the forelimbs to see if the horse stands squarely or if it toes out or in (Figs. 3-32A, B). In judging the forelimbs, most to least serious would be: an entire leg turned out, an entire leg turned in, toes

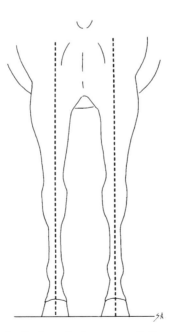

Fig. 3-31—Between the forelegs of a horse, a well-formed chest has an upside-down V shape, indicating proper musculature. Drawing by Sharon Ashby

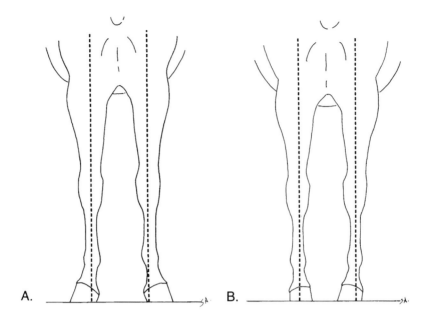

Figs. 3-32A, B—Toes turned out (A), and toes turned in (B). Drawings by Sharon Ashby

turned out, and toes turned in. The reason for this is that an entire leg out or in is worse than only toes out or in; and, because of the possibility of interference between the forelimbs, an out-turned position is worse than an in-turned position in the front legs. (In the rear end, however, an out-turned position is preferable because it allows the hocks to remain under the horse, while an in-turned position places the hocks to the outside of the horse and weakens its jumping effort.)

Look at the horse's right forefoot (in front of your left hand as you face the animal) and notice whether or not the foot is symmetrical, as it should be (Fig. 3-33). Continuing up the leg, look for sidebone, ringbone, osselets, windpuffs, and splints, since the new perspective may bring a previously overlooked abnormality to light. Viewed from the front, the bones in the legs should have substance, rather than looking thin and brittle. The forearms should be muscular and the legs should join smoothly with the chest. Once you have completed examination of the horse's right foreleg, go through the same procedure with the left foreleg.

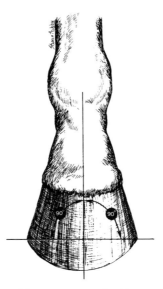

Fig. 3-33—A symmetrical foot. Drawing by Sharon Ashby

It is usually easier to find splints from the front view than from the side (Figs. 3-34A, B). When a splint is present, check for a "bench knee," a structural fault in which the cannon bone is offset toward the outside of the imaginary line (extending vertically from the point of the shoulder joint to the ground) that should be bisecting the foreleg (Fig. 3-35A). Lacking support from the cannon bone, the inside splint bone carries an abnormally heavy load, and the result is often inside splints.

Other structural faults found in this area are "knocked knees" and "bowed knees." In "knocked knees," the horse's forelegs bend in toward each other at the knees, so that the bones above and below the knees, as well as the knees themselves, lean inward (Fig. 3-35B). In "bowed knees," the forelegs bend outward at the knees, so the bones above and below the knees, as well as the knees themselves, lean outward (Fig. 3-35C). Both knocked knees and bowed knees cause the horse's weight to be distributed unequally down the legs; but knocked knees are more heavily penalized because they are usually accompanied by "toe-out" conformation, suggesting interference, while bowed knees are usually accompanied by "toe-in" conformation, which does not cause interference. Bench knees would be less penalized than the other two faults because it is a less radical deviation from the proper leg structure.

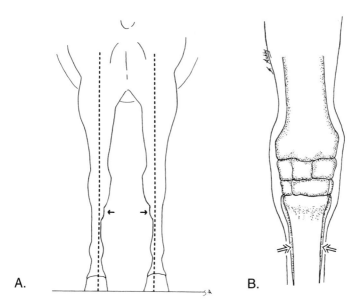

A.   B.

Figs. 3-34A, B—Since this horse has bench knees (see Fig. 3-35A), it is not surprising that there are splints on both forelegs (A). However, splints frequently occur in only one leg and may appear at other locations along the inner or outer splint bones, which are directly to the rear and sides of the cannon bone, as seen in this front view of a foreleg (B). Illustration A adapted from a drawing by Sharon Ashby/B by Sharon Ashby

From this front vantage point, look for a bulge on both sides of the upper portion of the knee. This silhouette, in which the bulge is usually larger on the inside than the outside of the knee, indicates an unclosed epiphyseal line (Fig. 3-35D). This is the least penalized of knee abnormalities, especially when the horses being judged are quite young, for the condition improves with age.

After examining the forelimbs, glance toward the hind legs to look for bone spavin, which may be easier to detect from this front view than from the prior oblique view (see Fig. 3-29). You may also find splints on the hind legs, although they are uncommon in the rear end.

Side View, Off Side

Move to the off side of the horse and stand far enough away to get an overview of the animal. You have already determined the general quality

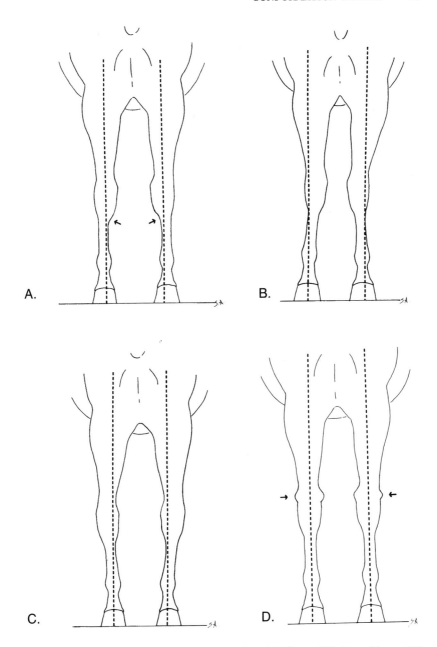

Figs. 3-35A, B, C, D—Bench knees (A); knocked knees (B); bowed knees (C); unclosed epiphyseal line (D). Drawings A, B, and C by Sharon Ashby/D adapted from a drawing by Sharon Ashby

and substance of the horse from the near side, but must check the off side for blemishes, such as a cup in the neck or a body scar.

Side View, Front Leg (Off Side)

Look for the same structural faults, defects, and blemishes outlined in Side View, Front Leg (Near Side), examining the outside of the foreleg on the off side of the horse, then the inside of the foreleg on the near side of the horse.

Side View, Hind Leg (Off Side)

Look for the same structural faults, defects, and blemishes outlined in Side View, Hind Leg (Near Side), examining the outside of the hind leg on the off side of the horse, then the inside of the hind leg on the near side of the horse.

Rear View

When the horse is viewed from the rear perspective, the point of the quarter, point of the hock, ergot, and center of the foot should be on the same vertical line (Fig. 3-36). You can easily detect two structural faults from the rear view: "bowed hocks" and "cow hocks." In "bowed hocks" the horse's hind legs bend outward, placing the hocks too far to the outside of the body (Fig. 3-37A). Since the hocks are not properly aligned beneath the haunches, the horse's jumping effort will be weak. In addition, when a horse has good conformation in front, but bowed hocks behind, the fault is likely to cause interference between front and hind limbs. Thirdly, the bowed hock formation causes excessive strain on the outside of the hind limbs, which may lead to unsoundness. These three problems—weak jumping effort, interference between front and hind limbs, and potential unsoundness—cause bowed hocks to be the most undesirable structural fault of the hind limbs.

"Cow hocks" is a fault in which the hocks are too close together and turned in so they point toward each other slightly, rather than being parallel (Fig. 3-37B). By placing excessive strain on the inside of the hind legs, cow hocks often cause bone spavin. In comparing structural faults of the hind end, cow hocks are preferable to sickle hocks and bowed hocks; but when cow hocks and sickle hocks appear together, as they often do,

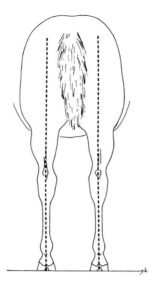

Fig. 3-36—In a correctly aligned horse, a vertical line connects the point of the quarter, point of the hock, ergot, and center of the foot. Drawing by Sharon Ashby

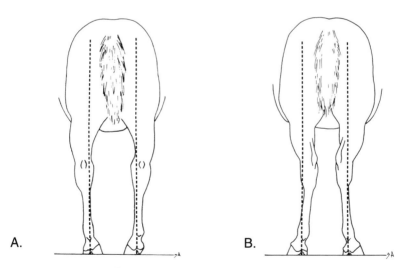

A.   B.

Figs. 3-37A, B—When a horse has bowed hocks, its toes tend to point inward (A). With the opposite formation, cow hocks, the horse's toes will generally be turned outward (B). Drawing A adapted from a drawing by Sharon Ashby/B by Sharon Ashby

this combination would be worse than sickle hocks alone, but still preferable to bowed hocks.

Each hock should appear well-developed and symmetrical from this rear view—a perspective that may further enforce findings you had from the side and front views concerning spavins, thoroughpins, curbs, or capped hocks. Run your eyes up the horse's left hind leg, then right hind leg, to check for any abnormalities already discussed that you might have missed when looking from other perspectives.

Once you have completed examination of the first horse in the line, go through the same procedure in judging each of the other horses. In all classes over obstacles, all horses being considered for an award must be jogged for soundness in the judge's order of preference prior to being judged for conformation. Two more entries than the number of ribbons offered must also be jogged if there are sufficient entries.

MODEL AND BREEDING CLASSES

Model and Breeding classes use the same basic criteria as Conformation classes, with one major exception. The jog, which is used only to determine soundness of the horse in Conformation classes, becomes very important in Model and Breeding classes as the only test of the horse's athletic ability. Since you haven't had the opportunity to watch the horses perform as you would in judging a Conformation class, you must pay close attention to the jog as an indicator of the accuracy of your judgement about the horses' conformation.

A horse that is built well should move well. You are looking for the good athlete—the horse that will be capable of turning in good performances over fences for many years to come—not for the overly fat, "hothouse" variety horse that has no blemishes but shows little promise as an athlete.

There are three systems of judging the way a horse moves, all of which were devised to examine the horse from the front, hind, and side views (Figs. 3-38 A, B, C,). In Figure 38A, the horse moves at a walk toward the judge, turns just in front of the judge and walks away, then turns again and jogs the length of the arena, giving the judge a final side view. In Figure 38B, the horse walks away from the judge on the first leg of the triangle, trots the second leg, then walks toward the judge on the third leg. In Figure 38C, the horse walks the first third of the length of the

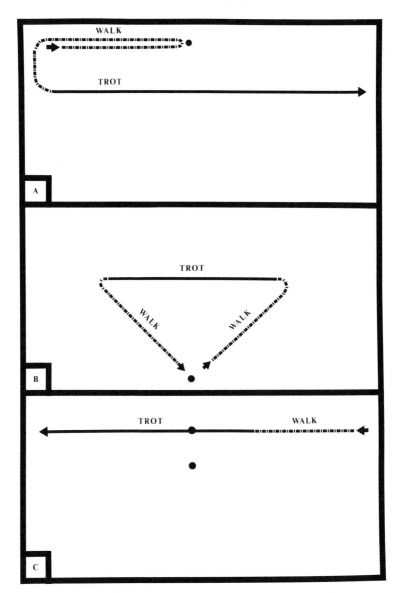

Figs. 3-38A, B, C—*The diagram shows patterns commonly used in the Hunter Breeding Division, with the dots representing the position of the judge during each pattern. Portions of the patterns performed at the walk are designated by interrupted lines, while trot segments are represented by solid lines. The third pattern, Fig. 3-38C, is often used in Futurity classes. Diagram by the author.*

ring, then trots the remaining two-thirds. The judge must start by standing on the line about halfway down the ring, move to the side as the horse
trots by, then move behind the horse as it trots away. This is the quickest
method, but it requires a judge capable of immediate, correct impressions and a lively step. The first method (Fig. 3-38A) is probably the
easiest for a novice judge.

The jog will be your only chance to see if the horse moves straight, has
a good length of stride, and demonstrates rhythm and coordination in its
motion. A good handler can minimize a horse's structural problems by
standing the horse in a position that shows the animal to its best advantage. But once that horse has to jog, its structural problems will become
apparent to the judge who has a keen eye to detect them. If the horse you
thought looked great turns out to paddle, be short-strided, or show some
other problem you didn't anticipate, then reconsider that horse's structure. The horse can only paddle if its foot isn't put on straight, and the
well-structured but short-strided horse may prove to be the obese animal
that is literally "too fat to move."

The jog, then, not only should be viewed as a test of soundness in a
Model or Breeding class, but should be considered as the ultimate test of
the theory you have used in judging the horses in the line-up. For this
reason, in Model and Breeding classes you judge the conformation of the
horses first, then jog the animals (or, in the case of broodmares and foals,
walk the animals), and finally move the horses into the proper position
for pinning.

It is important to keep in mind the intended use of the horse when
judging Breeding or Model classes. If your Breeding stock shows some
wear and tear from pasture life—such as a skinned place or the lack of a
polished coat or perfect weight—you are more forgiving than if the same
were true of your Model horse, which should show every sign of being at
its peak as a performance animal. When judging non-thoroughbreds, be
sure to judge the horse's appearance based on the task it will be required
to do. You would not pin high the heavy-set non-thoroughbred horse
with delicate thoroughbred legs, but would look for a horse that had
enough bone to support its heavier body.

When you judge a horse's conformation, your main consideration
should be how the horse's build will affect its ability to perform. If it is
Breeding stock you are judging, then you are considering the horse's
"performance" in terms of the quality of the traits it is capable of trans-

mitting to its offspring—that is, a well-balanced structure that promotes soundness and athletic ability.

If you are judging young horses in a Breeding or Model class, then "performance" is seen in more immediate terms. The jog should be crucial in your assessment of a young horse, for it is a major indicator of the animal's general athletic ability. After all, what is a horse worth that doesn't cover enough ground? You don't want to pin a horse high that has a limited future as a hunter.

4

EQUITATION ON THE FLAT

POSITION

Lower Body—From Heel to Pelvis

"Put your heels down!" is heard frequently in equitation lessons, not simply because this command produces a certain look, but because it causes the rider to be more securely fixed on his horse and gives him a position from which he can be more effective. When a rider's heels are down, he has allowed his weight to drop as far as it can and, consequently, he'll be much less likely to fall off than a person who doesn't exert this downward pressure.

It is important that the weight not only be distributed downward, but also that it be distributed equally on each side of the horse. When a rider leans to one side, causing his weight to shift off the horse's center, he is apt to fall off on the side he is leaning toward if the animal suddenly moves in the other direction. If he remains in the center of his horse, however, he'll be able to stay on through balance and not become unseated unless the horse has a major mishap, such as falling and rolling over.

The concept of staying on through balance and downward weight distribution becomes clearer if the rider is compared to a sack of grain laid over a donkey's back. The bag of grain has no muscle to hold it on and only stays in place because the grain has settled equally on each side of the donkey. So it is with a rider who sits in the middle of his horse and does not allow his weight to shift more to one side than the other.

Unequal weight distribution presents a balance problem not only for the rider but also for the horse. When a rider leans to one side, the horse invariably leans in that direction, too. Sometimes you'll see a competitor trying to push his horse away from his leg while he is leaning toward the leg he is using, so that his off-center upper body is moving the horse inward, counteracting the leg aid as it attempts to push the horse outward.

It is essential, then, for the rider to remain in the center of his horse, for the sake of his own and his horse's balance, and for him to keep his heels pressed down at all times, so he will be securely fixed on his mount no matter what problem arises. These two principles are so basic to the rider's safety that a person who does not sit centered on his horse or press his heels downward during all phases of competition should be heavily penalized in every level of equitation.

In addition to the ankle being pressed downward, it should also break slightly toward the horse's side, bringing the rider's calf into contact with the animal. A small portion of the sole of the boot will be visible to the judge because the side of the foot that is away from the horse is upturned as the inner side of the foot is depressed (Fig. 4-1). Although the rider's toe will naturally be farther from the horse than his heel, the toe should not be turned out so far that the rider uses the back of his calf, rather than the side of it, and lets his knee be pulled away from the saddle (Figs. 4-2A, B). This position—toe out, back of calf active, and knee out— should be heavily penalized because it takes the rider's security away as it pulls his leg from the saddle.

Lack of security in the leg causes a multitude of problems in the upper body. In general, a rider whose leg is thrust too far forward will be riding with his upper body "behind the motion," and, in, extreme cases, will be pounding on his horse's loins with his seat and pulling on the horse's mouth as he uses his reins to support his upper body (Fig. 4-3A). In contrast, a rider whose legs are too far back will be "ahead of the motion," and, in an extreme case, will be leaning on his hands to support his upper body and letting his horse move in an overly long frame because his hands and torso are rendered so passive that he cannot use them to balance the animal (Fig. 4-3B).

Since the leg thrust forward does not touch the horse's side, it is of no use in communicating with the animal; therefore, this leg position is se-

Fig. 4-1—Viewed from the side, the rider's knee and toe are on the same vertical line in this properly positioned leg. The rider's calf is against the horse, and only a small portion of the sole of the boot is visible—the downward and inward pressure of the foot on the stirrup causing the side of the foot that is away from the horse to be turned up slightly. Photograph by Suzie Richburg

A.

B.

Figs. 4-2A, B—In this incorrectly positioned leg (A), the rider's toe and knee turn away from the horse and the back of the lower leg is in contact with the animal's side. In contrast (B), this correctly positioned leg is snug against the saddle and horse. The inner knee bone is in contact with the saddle, the inside of the lower leg is against the horse's side, and the toe is turned out only slightly. Photographs by Suzie Richburg

A.

B.

Figs. 4-3A, B—The rider's lower leg has slipped forward (A), causing her upper body to be thrust behind the motion of the horse at the trot and her seat and hand to be abusive. At the other extreme, the rider's leg has slipped back-ward (B), causing her upper body to be thrust ahead of the motion and her hands to be passive—that is, her hands can only be used to support her torso, not to control the horse. Photograph A by Suzie Richburg/B by A. O. White, Jr.

verely penalized. A leg drawn back too far is weak, but is not penalized as seriously because it can communicate somewhat with the horse. Compared with these major leg faults, the ideal rider's leg is positioned just behind the horse's girth, with the steady leg providing a sound foundation for the upper body (Fig. 4-4).

Finally, there are riders whose legs appear to be in the correct position when viewed from the side, but who from the oblique or rear view can be seen not to have contact with the horse (Figs. 4-5A, B). These riders appear balanced as long as their horses are cooperative, but will be pulled out of position if their horses become strong. This is often the case with a rider who is on a high-strung horse and is afraid to add leg pressure for fear of the horse becoming even more keyed up. Although the rider may appear to be positioned correctly from the side, he is actually committing a serious fault in not having his leg on the horse, for the leg is one of the prime sources of control of the animal. It is preferable, however, for the

Fig. 4-4—*In a position called "at the girth" (that is, positioned just behind the girth), the rider's leg provides a sound foundation for the upper body. Photograph by Pennington Galleries*

rider to have this fault of seeming to have a good leg position, but not actually having the leg on the horse, than to have either of the other two faults mentioned—that is, leg kicked forward or drawn back too far. This is because in the case of the well-positioned, but inactive leg, the rider is at least supporting his own weight from his leg, and his upper body is not being thrown out of balance with the horse. A rider can learn to use his leg properly at this point, whereas riders who have their legs too far forward or back must first correct these errors and the many accompanying faults before they can learn to use the leg properly as an aid.

In summary, the major faults of the lower leg, ranging from most to least serious, are: legs too far forward; legs too far back; and legs that appear to have proper angles when viewed from the side, but are not actually against the horse. This last fault can best be seen during the canter, in which the motion of the horse's stride will generally cause the rider's leg to swing back and forth.

 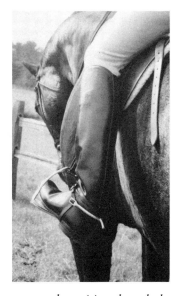

A. B.

Figs. 4-5A, B—Although this rider's leg (A) appears to be positioned much the same as in Figure 4-1, there is a major difference. You can see by the ray of sunlight behind this rider's heel that her leg is not on the horse's side. The error is much more obvious when the same leg position is photographed from a rear perspective (B). Photographs by Suzie Richburg

Now move up to the knee, thigh, and buttocks to consider faults that may occur in these areas. The knee should remain close to the saddle at all times, acting in conjunction with the rider's calf and thigh to produce a secure and effective leg. When a rider's knee is pulled away from the saddle, you should look for two possible causes: either the rider is improperly using the back, rather than side, of his calf against the horse (Fig. 4-6), or the rider's conformation does not fit his animal's.

A long-legged rider on an animal too narrow-bodied for him will often exhibit this fault of the knee being away from the saddle, for he finds he must turn loose at the knee in order to press his lower leg against his horse. In the case of a mismatched horse and rider, it is preferable to see a gap at the knee than the other option the rider would have, which would be to keep his knee close to the saddle and not have his lower leg on the horse. Of course, the answer to this dilemma is that the rider should compete on an animal that suits him and not on one too small or too thin; but if you are faced with pinning two riders with this problem of being poorly mounted, the one who keeps his lower leg on the horse, but has his knee off, should place above the one who has his knee close to the saddle, but his lower leg off the horse's side.

Moving upward visually, notice the rider's thighs and buttocks at various gaits. At the walk, you may see a rider using these portions of his body to push his horse forward, rather than motivating the horse properly with his legs. This obvious movement in the rider's seat is penalized because the thighs and buttocks should be following the horse's movement at the walk, rather than creating the impulsion.

At the sitting trot, many competitors have a problem keeping their thighs and buttocks relaxed, and they either bounce each step or slow their horses down to keep from bouncing. A well-positioned, relaxed rider who knows how to shorten and lengthen his horse's frame will not have to cut the animal's pace in order to sit the trot, but will be able to collect the horse—while maintaining the rhythm of the working trot—and sit quite comfortably and still, having altered the horse's center of gravity back toward his seat through collection of the animal's frame. Tension in the thighs, buttocks, and stomach, as well as a lack of knowledge concerning collection, is the cause of bouncing; and riders usually try to conquer this problem by gripping with their legs to hold themselves on, rather than letting their weight and balance follow the horse's movements and effortlessly keep them in the saddle.

Fig. 4-6—When a rider's knee and toe turn out, the back of the lower leg— rather than the inside of it—comes into contact with the horse. In this position, the rider must grip with the calf to keep the leg still, since it is impossible to receive any stability from the saddle if the knee is pulled away from it. Photograph by A. O. White, Jr.

In judging the sitting trot, call for a "working trot sitting"—not a "slow, sitting trot"—and penalize riders who evade the test by cutting the pace. If you request that stirrups be dropped for this test, ask the riders to cross them, so the irons won't bang against the horses' sides (Fig. 4-7).

At the sitting trot, the rider's pelvis angle should be slightly closed— just a couple of degrees in front of the vertical, the same as for the walk. If

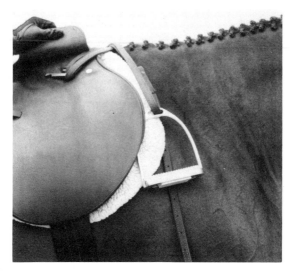

Fig. 4-7—If a rider's stirrups are properly crossed, as in this photograph, the leathers will lie flat under the thighs and not cause bruises. When requesting work without stirrups, give the riders time to cross the leathers so the stirrup irons won't bang against the horses' sides. Photograph by A. O. White, Jr.

the rider allows his upper body to go behind the vertical, he should be penalized for the forced appearance that accompanies this error; and an even greater penalty must go to the rider who is at the other extreme, closing his pelvis too far forward so he is ahead of the motion, with his upper body rendered ineffective (Fig. 4-8).

When asked to perform the posting trot, the rider will close his pelvis at an angle no greater than 20 degrees in front of the vertical. This hip closure will cause the rider to be posting on his thighs and crotch, rather than on his buttocks (Fig. 4-9).

At the canter, the pelvis returns to the angle of the walk and sitting trot—only a few degrees in front of the vertical—as the rider's body adjusts from the horizontal motion of the horse's trot to the more vertical motion of the canter (Fig. 4-10). When the rider's pelvis angle opens from the position of the posting trot to that of the canter, he is no longer on his crotch, and his buttocks and thighs can be used to absorb the shock of the canter. Tension in the buttocks and thighs will result in noticeable bouncing of the rider during each stride. This fault should be penalized for it shows that the rider's base of support—his seat—is inef-

Fig. 4-8—During work without stirrups, the rider's leg should be positioned as usual—ankle flexed, calf against horse, knee close to saddle. The angle of the upper body at the various gaits will also be the same without stirrups as with them. At the sitting trot (pictured here), the torso is only a couple of degrees in front of the vertical—inclined just enough that the rider isn't behind the motion. Photograph by Suzie Richburg

Fig. 4-9—At the working trot rising, this rider's body is inclined 20 degrees in front of the vertical. The pelvis may be slightly more open (closer to the vertical) and still be correct, but it should never be closed more than 20 degrees at the posting trot. Photograph by Pennington Galleries.

Fig. 4-10—*At the canter, the rider's upper body should only be a few degrees in front of the vertical. Photograph by Pennington Galleries.*

fective, as opposed to a deep, relaxed seat that would indicate support for the rider's upper body and control of the horse.

Although a good rider's thighs and buttocks are relaxed, this does not mean they are physically unfit, for a rider with a weak seat slides back and forth in the saddle as the horse moves, while a fit rider's thighs and buttocks are sunken into the saddle, so horse and rider are at one during the walk, sitting trot, and canter.

Upper Body—From the Pelvis Up

Next, consider the upper body: back, shoulders, neck, head, eyes, and arms. Take note of the torso angulation at each of the gaits and penalize riders who are either behind or ahead of the motion of their horses. As previously mentioned, if the rider's balance problem begins in the leg, a forward leg position accompanied by a behind-the-motion upper body is worse than a leg too far back accompanied by an in-front-of-the-motion upper body. If, however, the rider's leg is positioned correctly and is effective, but the rider's upper body is either ahead of or behind the motion, the degree of penalty for the improper torso angulation would depend on the adverse effect on the horse's performance or the indication of a weakness in the rider's aids.

Besides counting off for these general balance faults, look for specific upper-body faults, such as a loose back, roached back, swayback, rounded shoulders, shoulders forced back too far, a neck stretched forward, a set jaw, or a head cocked to one side. The worst of the errors that can occur in the rider's back is a "loose back," which is a slinging movement in the rider's waist as the horse moves forward. This fault at the trot is usually caused by the rider not stretching upward in his back on an animal that has a particularly springy trot, so that the horse's movement slings the rider's body, making him look weak and sloppy.

At the canter, the loose back indicates that the rider is fixing his arm in an effort to restrict the horse's length of stride, but the arm is not reinforced by a strong back (which may be traced even further to the lack of a secure leg position). As the rider tries to restrain his animal, the horse is maintaining the lengthy stride by pulling the rider's waist forward. If the rider could keep his back still, he could correctly perform the half-halt, and the animal would go in a more collected frame and not produce this loose-backed appearance in the rider. A loose back should be penalized heavily, for just as a poor leg position indicates an ineffectual leg, the loose back indicates an ineffectual back.

Another fault that may be found in the back is a "roached back" (also called a "rounded back"). This fault is a combination of buttocks that are tucked under and shoulders that are rounded (Fig. 4-11). Although the roached back can be effective when accompanied by an extremely short stirrup—as for steeplechasing or flat racing—it is not a strong position when accompanied by the proper equitation-length stirrup, which hits just below the rider's ankle when he drops his stirrups and hangs his leg in a relaxed manner. Since the roached back is both ineffective and unattractive, it is heavily penalized.

A third fault found in this area is the "swayback" (also called a "hollow back"), characterized by the rider closing his hip angle too much and carrying his buttocks too far behind him and his shoulders too far back (Fig. 4-12). The acute angle of the pelvis causes the rider to lose much of the power of his back that is necessary for control in a variety of movements, from the half-halt to sharp turns on tight jumping courses. The swayback is definitely preferable to the loose back because at least it is stationary and has some strength. In comparing the swayback and

Fig. 4-11—Rounding her shoulders and tucking her buttocks under, this rider has a "roached back." Both ineffective and unattractive, the roached back is heavily penalized. Photograph by Suzie Richburg

Fig. 4-12—With shoulders forced backward and buttocks protruding toward the rear of the saddle, the rider displays a "swayback." This fault makes the rider look stiff and inhibits proper use of the back during half-halts. Photograph by Suzie Richburg

roached back on the flat, although both of these faults show a weakness, the swayback generally is pinned higher because it is less unattractive visually and is usually accompanied by fewer position faults.

"Rounded shoulders," which may appear without the rider having his entire back roached, is a position fault usually found in long-waisted riders, who may also carry themselves with rounded shoulders when off a horse (Fig. 4-13). Ideally, the back should be used subtly to keep the animal balanced—for example, the back should act in conjunction with the rider's hands and legs during half-halts or on tight turns. In contrast, riders with rounded shoulders are limited in their use of the back and are not in as much control of their animals as those who keep the back straight and are able to use it fully.

The opposite of rounded shoulders is a position in which the rider has "forced-back shoulders" (Fig. 4-14). Usually, this fault is present in a rider who is either swaybacked, as mentioned before, or who naturally has rounded shoulders and is forcing them back in order to have what he believes to be the correct appearance in an equitation class. Again, the

Fig. 4-13—"Rounded shoulders" weaken the effectiveness of the rider's back and detract from an elegant appearance. Photograph by Suzie Richburg

Fig. 4-14—*Young riders often respond to a coach's command to "sit up straight" by forcing their shoulders back.*

Fig. 4-15—*The "neck stretched forward" and "set jaw" diminish the upper body's effectiveness and make an unattractive picture. Photograph by Suzie Richburg*

shoulders being out of line with the rest of the upper body causes the back to lose some of its strength; however, this forced-back position of the shoulders is preferable to rounded shoulders because it is a somewhat stronger position from which the rider can work.

Moving up to the area of the neck and head, look for a "neck stretched forward," out of line with the rest of the rider's torso, and a "set jaw," in which the rider has his jaw thrust forward (Fig. 4-15).

Since the neck and head are upward extensions of the rider's torso, any excess inclination of them should be penalized for diminishing the strength of the upper body. When viewed from the side, the rider's head and neck should be in line with the upper body as though the rider's torso had been pulled upward from the top of the head by a string. In addition, a rider should not cock his head to one side or the other, for this, too, is a distortion of the straight and strong upper body desirable in a rider (Fig. 4-16).

Fig. 4-16—When the rider's head is cocked to one side, the upper body weight shifts in that direction, too. The degree of penalty for a "cocked head" depends on related errors in the rider's position and the horse's performance.
Photograph by Suzie Richburg

You should also notice the rider's use of his eyes during an equitation class on the flat. Throughout the class, the rider should be using his eyes to look slightly ahead of where he and the horse are so that he can anticipate: (1) the path he will take according to where other horses are in the ring or where jumps, standards, or other objects within the ring are set; and (2) any adjustments he might need to make concerning extension, collection, bending, and so forth, according to the specific tests, the shape and size of the ring, and the traffic pattern of the other competitors.

The rider should turn his head slightly toward the direction of travel on corners and face straight ahead on the straight sides of the ring. If he exaggerates the turning of his head while traveling around corners so that he is almost looking over his shoulder, he should be penalized for "looking too far ahead," a fault that indicates he is thinking too far ahead and is not concerned enough with the horse's immediate performance (Fig. 4-17). The rider must be capable of concentrating on what he is currently doing as well as on what he will have to do—dealing suffi-

Fig. 4-17—This rider is looking too far ahead on a corner during a flat class. Instead of gazing over her shoulder, she should be looking only slightly ahead of where she and the horse are, as in Figure 4-9. Photograph by Suzie Richburg

ciently with the present and planning sufficiently for the future—if he wants to succeed in the show ring (or anywhere else, for that matter!).

Worse than "looking too far ahead" is "not looking soon enough." A rider who doesn't look soon enough is so absorbed in what is presently happening that he doesn't look ahead of where he is to plan for what he'll have to do next. Ideally, a rider should use peripheral vision to get an idea of what is going on everywhere in the ring and should use this knowledge to pick the best paths to show himself to the judge and stay out of trouble. By noticing a group of horses misbehaving in another area of the ring, the competitor can determine approximately how long it will take these horses to catch up to him. Then he can plan to avoid the impending trouble by circling behind the group—giving them another circuit around the ring before they catch up once again—or by moving to the rail or inside track of the ring to let the horses pass, with this decision depending on which path the horses are taking when the rider views their problem. Sometimes escape from this type of situation is impossible, especially when the class is packed. However, a smart rider will keep his eyes active enough to avoid most of these situations and, in addition, will plan passes in front of the judge by looking for holes in the herd into which he can slip and be seen alone, to his best advantage.

Besides the rider's eyes being used to plan ahead, they can also be subtly used to check leads or diagonals. After the beginner stage, a rider should not have to look down to check a lead or diagonal; he should be able to feel it. However, if a rider is uncertain without visual assurance, he can keep his head in normal position and cast a quick glance downward at the horse's shoulder (Figs. 4-18A, B). Glancing for a moment should not be penalized in equitation classes; but when the rider tilts his head downward or leans over to look for a lead or diagonal, he should be penalized for lacking sensitivity and sophistication.

Finally, consider the rider's hands, the effectiveness of which will be greatly determined by the rider's leg, seat, and use of his upper body. As mentioned before, if the rider's leg position is incorrect, it will generally be evident in his upper body. For the rider with his legs kicked forward, the hands will generally be used as a support mechanism as the rider attempts to pull himself up at the posting trot, rather than pushing himself up from his leg (see Fig. 4-3A). For the rider with his legs too far behind him, the hands will be used to support his upper body weight as he leans forward onto them to catch his balance (see Fig. 4-3B). These are the worst hand faults—the first being abusive to the animal's mouth,

A.

B.

Figs. 4-18A, B—Compare the rider who checks the diagonal properly by glancing (A) with the one who incorrectly tilts her head to look (B). Ideally, the rider should be able to check diagonals and leads through feel alone. Photographs by Suzie Richburg

and, consequently, the more serious of the two; and the second exhibiting a completely passive hand that is unable to control the animal. When I call these two hand faults "the worst," I am putting them in perspective with other hand faults the rider could commit without intentionally trying to abuse the horse. Of course, a rider who jerks his horse in the mouth or wrings the bit from side to side in an intentionally abusive manner is in an entirely different category. These types of abusive behavior are not to be tolerated by the judge, and if they are considered abusive to the point of "cruelty," you should deal with them accordingly, as provided for in the *AHSA Rule Book.*

Next in the line of hand faults is what is commonly called a "fixed hand." This term is used for riders who do not follow the motion of the horse's head during the gaits, but who set their hands in an immobile position. The look of the fixed hand is one of rigidity, in which the rider appears to be holding the horse's head in place (Fig. 4-19). (This fault

Fig. 4-19—If a rider fixes his hands on a horse that pulls, the animal will continue to travel on its forehand, counterbalancing its front end against the rider's weight. When intimidated by a pulling horse, a rider may remove leg and seat pressure, in an effort to placate the animal, and lean on the hand to support the upper body. This position is insecure, ineffective, and unattractive. Photograph by Suzie Richburg

could more appropriately be called a "fixed arm," for it is not the hand alone that is unresponsive as much as the entire arm, which should be following the motion of the horse's head.) The fixed hand is often seen in a rider on a high-strung animal as he attempts to restrain the horse from getting faster. In this case, the horse will try to escape the fixed hand either by pulling its head in toward its chest, behind the bit, or by fighting the rider's hands, trying to pull the reins out of them. Accompanying faults seen in riders with a fixed arm on a tense horse are: an insecure leg position as the rider attempts to hold his legs away from the horse's sides in hope the animal may slow down from the lack of leg pressure; the rider holding his seat out of the saddle as he tries to avoid any pressure against the horse's back that might cause it to go even faster; and a low hand as the rider attempts to balance himself on his hands, since he doesn't have the leg or seat security from which to support his upper body.

The problem of the fixed arm is not restricted to riders on tense horses, but is seen also in riders on dull horses that pull. The dull horse that leans heavily on its front end will often cause a rider with a weak leg, seat, and upper body to fix his hands to support the horse's front-end weight. In this case, the rider is lacking the means to half-halt his animal and make it carry its own body weight. Although this type of horse is the opposite from the tense one mentioned above, its rider may have many of the same position faults—insecure leg, seat out of the saddle, and a low hand.

In summary, hand faults found in an equitation class are, from most to least serious: hanging on a horse's mouth for balance (abusive hands); leaning on the hands for balance (passive hands); and fixing the hands, rather than following the motion of the horse's head. In high-level equitation classes, riders will have their horses in a more collected frame than competitors in lower levels. In order to achieve this collection, the rider performs a series of half-halts that require a momentary fixing of the hands and cause the horse to have less motion in its head and neck. Thus, a hand that can properly produce the half-halt (in conjunction with the leg) should not be mistaken for the insensitive, fixed hand that sets against the horse for lack of a proper half-halt. The greatest indication that the rider has a fixed hand is the horse's reaction. Even if the horse's head is positioned low and the neck is slightly flexed, if the animal travels with its mouth open, pulls on the bit, or drops behind the bit, you should check to see if a fixed hand is the cause.

Ideally, the hands should be persuasive with an animal, so the rider can accomplish what he wants without the animal looking distressed. The hand should not be severe, causing the horse to react abruptly, nor should it be so passive that it allows the horse to travel unchecked on a long frame. Instead, the hand should subtly balance the horse in all gaits with such finesse that it is an "invisible aid."

In proper position, the hands are just over and slightly in front of the withers, and, when viewed from the side, in a direct line from the rider's elbow to the horse's mouth (Fig. 4-20). If the rider's reins are too long, he will not have sufficient control of his horse; this is especially noticeable when the horse becomes "strong" and the rider ends up with his hands in his stomach as he tries to slow the animal down. If the reins are held too

Fig. 4-20—In proper position, the hands are just over and slightly in front of the withers and in a direct line from the rider's elbow to the horse's mouth. The forearms and wrists should be straight, and the thumbs just inside the vertical and only a couple of inches apart. Photograph by Suzie Richburg

A.

B.

Figs. 4-21A, B—An overly short rein causes the rider to lean forward (A); excessively long reins result in the hands being against the stomach when the rider tries to half-halt (B). Photograph A by Pennington Galleries/B by Suzie Richburg

short, the rider's upper body and seat will be pulled ahead of the horse's motion (Figs. 4-21A, B).

The long rein results in an uncontrolled performance at worst or an imprecise one at best; while an overly short rein—usually associated with an aggressive or anxious rider—draws the rider's seat out of the saddle, so he cannot feel the subtleties of the horse's movements, such as the sequence of the feet, lateral suppleness, and impulsion. The degree of penalty for reins too short or too long depends upon the effect each has on the rider's position and on the horse's performance.

Conclusion

From the discussion of faults in the lower and upper body, some generalities can be derived concerning position errors. First, the most serious position errors are those that negatively affect the rider's balance. Second, since a rider's balance and effectiveness are greatly determined by his leg position, the worst position errors are those that allow the lack of secure contact between the rider's legs and the horse's sides.

Many riders attempt to communicate with their horses predominantly through their hands, rather than through their legs, and find themselves limited in what they can accomplish. If the rider cannot keep his legs against the horse at all times without the horse overreacting, then he has chosen the wrong animal for the job and should look for a mount on which he can compete without being intimidated into removing his leg. As a judge, you are not supposed to justify the lack of leg contact by thinking, "Well, the rider is on a hot horse." Instead, you should penalize this lack of leg contact severely and leave it to the competitor either to solve the problem on his current mount or else compete on another horse.

Having taken note of the general balance of each rider and, specifically, how leg position affects this balance, consider the interaction of all body parts and pin riders who are the most securely positioned, balanced, coordinated, sensitive to their animals, and disciplined in their attitude toward performance. Riders should not be smiling throughout a flat class—as they are sometimes advised to do by misinformed coaches—but should have a look of concentration on their faces, for you are considering skill and quality of performance, not personality.

PERFORMANCE

General Observations

"Performance" is what the rider is able to accomplish with his horse based on security of position and proper use of his aids. Just as the rider must exhibit a look of concentration on his work, the horse also should have this disciplined appearance throughout the performance. The animal should be moving ahead in a forthright manner, minding its own business rather than looking out of the ring or paying attention to other horses within the arena. If a horse becomes somewhat distracted during a flat class—lifting its head for a moment—but the rider gets the horse back to work, the penalty should not be great, unless the distraction results in bolting, breaking gait, or some other major fault during the class.

In judging performance, note how riders deal with problems that crop up during the class. For instance, if two riders are having trouble with spooky horses, the rider who is assertive and works his horse forward out of the problem should receive less penalty than the rider who is passive and lets the horse continue to shy away from objects and drop behind the leg.

Especially in judging beginner classes, consider not only what the rider is able to do, but also what he is trying to do. For example, in a division of very young riders, one who is obviously trying to bend his horse, but is unable to get it bent properly from head to tail, should place above one who is seemingly unaware that his animal is supposed to be bent and is content to let his horse lean to the inside on every corner. Although neither rider performed well, the one who showed knowledge of bending and kept trying to correct his animal should place above the one who was unaware of his error. If a third rider in the class is able to bend his horse correctly, he will, of course, be given highest place, since the reward for good intentions should not exceed the reward for a good performance.

Impulsion and Cadence

One of the most important aspects of performance, either on the flat or over fences, is impulsion. Impulsion is not the speed or "pace" at which the horse is going, but is the push power or "thrust" the animal has as it takes each step (Fig. 4-22A, B). Accompanying this thrust, the horse must have a steady cadence in each of the gaits. Impulsion, then, is best described as "rhythmic thrust."

A.

B.

Fig. 4-22A, B—During the sitting trot, this horse has lost its impulsion and is traveling above the bit (A). In contrast (B), this horse is moving with impulsion, engaging its hocks and staying on the bit. Photographs by Pennington Galleries

At the walk, the rider's legs should cause the horse to keep a definite forward rhythm. This is sometimes referred to as a "marching rhythm," although I find this terminology misleading because I associate it with a high-stepping movement, which the walk is not. However, the word "march" also suggests a regular cadence; and it is in this sense that the horse's proper walk is compared to a march.

In judging any flat classes, you should consider the cadence of the gaits to be very important. Riders who treat the walk as a "time out" should be penalized for not correctly performing the test. This penalty should carry the same weight as that for riders who slow their mounts down for the sitting trot, for in both cases, the test is performed very badly.

In all gaits, the horse should be pushing from its hind legs in a regular cadence; if a horse plods or rushes, penalize the rider for not creating and maintaining the proper impulsion.

On the Bit

Getting a horse "on the bit" begins with the rider creating impulsion in the animal's rear end, for when the hocks are engaged, the horse will seek the bit with its head and neck. By half-halting the animal periodically, the rider can restrict it from elongating its frame, so the horse will remain on the bit in a medium frame, rather than extending into a long frame in reaction to the rider's maintenance of leg pressure (Fig. 4-23).

Once the horse is on the bit, it should stay there, not drop "behind the bit" by bringing its head in toward its chest. Though both a horse that is behind the bit and one that is "pulling" present a problem, the animal that travels behind the bit is committing the greater fault, for it is entirely evading the hand by not moving forward from the leg onto the bit (Figs. 4-24A, B).

Though a pulling horse often causes its rider to be drawn forward into a hunched position, if the rider uses his aids properly, he can half-halt the animal and cause it to carry its own body weight and not pull. A horse behind the bit, however, is typically an anxious animal that will keep drawing its head back into its chest to avoid hand contact; and if the rider is persistent in driving the horse to the bit, the animal often becomes more upset and its high-strung appearance ruins the performance. Therefore, although a rider may sit nicely on a horse that is trying to stay behind the bit, the problem will surface whenever the rider needs to have

Fig. 4-23—Traveling "on the bit" and in a medium frame at the canter, this horse appears to be well-schooled, obedient, and balanced. (Basically, the rider's position is very good. The only improvements would be straightening the wrist and bringing the toe in slightly.) Photograph by Pennington Galleries

the horse on the bit for more difficult movements, such as the counter canter or a lengthening of stride at the working trot or working canter. In these tests, a horse that can be half-halted and lightened is preferable to one that refuses to go to the bit. However, you must consider the particular situation and pin accordingly.

For instance, if a heavy horse pulls its rider out of position and travels strung out, certainly this is worse than a horse slightly behind the bit that stays in an adequate frame for the tests and allows its rider to maintain a balanced position. If, however, the situation is reversed, so that the heavy horse is dealt with properly by its rider and remains in an adequate frame with sufficient impulsion, while the horse behind the bit has its head drawn into its chest and is just about to blow up, then the heavy horse's performance would be preferable.

Worse than a horse that pulls or drops behind the bit is one that raises its head in the air, escaping "above the bit" (Fig. 4-25). This fault is seen mostly in horses whose necks are built upright, for the steep conforma-

A.

B.

*Figs. 4-24A, B—At the hand gallop, this horse is "dropping behind the bit,"
bringing its head in toward its chest rather than moving forward willingly
from the rider's leg into the hand (A). In contrast, the pulling horse is
successfully drawing the rider forward, out of the saddle and onto her hands,
during the hand gallop (B). The combination of "standing in the stirrups" and
rounding the shoulders diminishes the effectiveness of this rider's back and
prevents her from half-halting the horse successfully. Photograph A by A. O.
White, Jr./B by Suzie Richburg*

Fig. 4-25—This horse is lifting its head to escape the rider's hands. An animal that goes "above the bit" is severely penalized because the fault indicates evasion of the rider's legs and seat, as well as hands. Photograph by Pennington Galleries

tion encourages the horse to use an upward route whenever it wants to avoid hand pressure. However, when seen in a horse with a properly constructed neck, the raised head usually signifies an emotional reaction to the rider—such as anger or panic—for if the horse were mildly resisting the hands, it would tend either to pull on or drop behind the bit because of its conformational predisposition, rather than take the more uncomfortable upward route. You should severely penalize horses that go "above the bit," because they are evading the rider's hands, legs (the horse will not move forward from the leg to the bit), and seat (an upraised head causes the horse's back to invert, making it impossible for the rider to sit comfortably).

Bending

Besides looking for proper impulsion and the horse being "on the bit," notice whether or not the rider bends the horse around the corners of the ring. "Bending" is the part of performance on the flat that demonstrates the rider's ability to make his horse supple from side to side (while impulsion reflects the rider's ability to create forward rhythmic thrust of the horse's energy). When a rider cannot bend his horse, he is at a great disadvantage in competition because the unbent animal is poorly balanced around corners, including not only the ends of the ring, but also any tests that involve curves, such as circles, half-turns, or serpentines.

A properly bent horse is molded around the rider's inside leg according to the shape of the turn. That is, the animal is bent from head to tail to the same degree as the acuteness of the curve it is negotiating. In basic terms, when the animal is circling to the left, its entire body is bent to the left—its head is turned slightly in the direction in which it is traveling; its body is bent from head to tail; and its inside legs are on one track, while its outside legs are on another (Fig. 4-26).

At the other extreme is the horse that travels around corners as stiff as a board—with its head "cranked" to the outside and its shoulders and haunches leaning toward the middle of the ring. This lack of bending is heavily penalized because it restricts the horse's vision, shortens its stride, and threatens its balance and, consequently, the safety of the rider. Even a very young rider should be aware of the importance of bending and be penalized for holding a pony's head toward the rail with an outside hand, rather than holding the animal's body to the rail with pressure from the inside leg (Fig. 4-27).

Smooth Transitions

Another concept that should be familiar to riders in even the young age groups is the smooth transition between gaits. In younger riders, poor transitions are often blatantly apparent during upward changes of gait, whereas more experienced riders, usually adept at upward transitions, are more likely to commit errors in downward changes.

The biggest problem for beginners is the transition into the canter, whether it be from the trot or walk. Many young riders hang their upper bodies over one of the shoulders of their horses to try to make them take the correct lead. This is a major mistake, for the competitor is attempting to engage the canter with his upper body instead of his leg and, by leaning forward, is thrusting his own weight on the horse's front end, making it more difficult for the horse to lift its forehand into the canter sequence. As mentioned several times before, the rider's leg is all important, and a fault that involves an ineffective leg is a serious one.

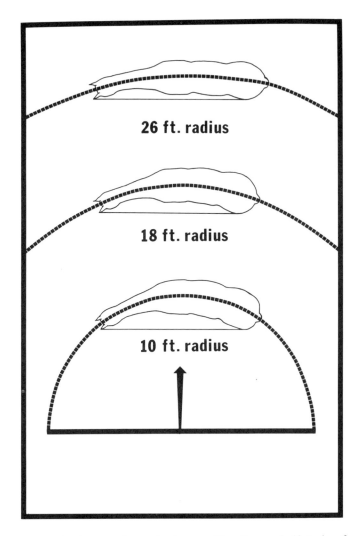

26 ft. radius

18 ft. radius

10 ft. radius

Fig. 4-26—The diagram shows the degrees of bending on half-circles of varying radii. Although each horse's spine appears to match the pattern of the bend, this is a visual deception. The part of the spine from the withers to the dock is restricted by the shoulder, rib, and hip bones, and thus is not as flexible as the spine in front of the withers. Although this restriction prohibits the backbone from being bent uniformly from head to tail, the horse will appear uniformly bent because the soft tissues surrounding the shoulder and hip permit some lateral flexibility which allows the outside plane of the rib cage to follow the pattern of the turn. Diagram by the author

Fig. 4-27—This is a familiar picture: the rider trying to hold the pony to the rail with an outside leading rein, while inadvertently drawing the pony into the ring by leaning to check the lead. Although the picture is not in good focus, it's such a good example of this often seen error that I couldn't resist using it.

With advanced riders, however, the problem of smoothly performing an upward transition usually has been conquered, and the horse requires but a simple leg aid, accompanied by a balancing hand, to engage the canter. In downward transitions, however, riders are often concerned with promptness at the expense of smoothness, and they abruptly "slam on the brakes" into the downward transition, so the horse stops with its haunches out behind, its nose poked out in front, and most of its weight thrust on its forehand.

A poor downward transition is a serious fault at the advanced level, for it means that the rider abandons his leg when he wants his horse to slow down, and the passive leg aid will pervade the animal's performance both on the flat and over fences. Correctly, the rider should prepare for the downward transition by performing a half-halt—that is, by momentarily adding both hand and leg pressure to collect the animal—

then he should perform a series of half-halts (with the number of half-halts depending on the particular horse) to further slow the animal down, so the transition is smooth and balanced.

In comparing a poor upward transition with a poor downward transition, the poor upward transition is the greater fault, for it is a more basic command. For instance, if a rider asks his horse to canter from the trot and the horse trots faster and faster before breaking into the canter, this would be an elementary-level mistake on the part of the rider, who did not teach his horse to respond immediately from the leg aid. As has been stressed throughout this text, it is essential for the horse to move willingly forward from the rider's legs, for any hesitancy to do so (such as balking, refusing at a fence, or rearing) spells danger for the rider.

An abrupt downward transition indicates either that the rider is allowing the horse to drop behind his leg, or that the rider must be rough in order to control his horse. Unless the horse is out of control, however, an abrupt but prompt transition is better than a very late transition.

Flexion and Collection

"Flexion" is the contraction of the horse's neck that results from the rider pressing the horse onto the bit with his legs and half-halting the horse with his hands. When a horse is flexed, its head moves inward toward the vertical and its neck becomes more arched. This aspect of flexion is visually obvious to the novice, who often assumes that this appearance is caused by hand pressure alone. As a result, uneducated riders attempt to hold the horse's head down with a fixed hand in order to achieve a flexed look (Fig. 4-28).

Nothing could be less correct than this forced flexion, for flexion properly starts with the horse's engine—its haunches—not with its mouth. When a horse moves forward with impulsion, it is thrusting its energy into the rider's hands. If unrestricted by half-halts, the horse will extend its stride or break into an upper gait. By half-halting, the rider can ask the horse to elevate the front portion of its body, rather than let the horse drive its weight downward into the ground and travel "strung out" on the forehand (Figs. 4-29A, B).

When a half-halt is properly accomplished, the horse maintains its impulsion from behind, but collects itself in front, and during this accordion-like procedure, the neck takes on a flexed appearance. Half-halts

Fig. 4-28—Leaning backward to set her upper body weight against the horse, the rider is forcing the animal to flex its neck. When a horse's head goes behind the vertical, as in this photograph, the neck is "overflexed." The open mouth indicates the animal's discomfort. Photograph by Suzie Richburg

should create lightness in the horse as it carries its own weight rather than leaning on the rider's hands to support the weight of its head and neck.

The entire picture of the horse traveling with its hocks well under its body and its neck flexed is called "collection" (that is, the animal is "collected" from both ends), whereas the contracted appearance of the horse's neck alone is "flexion." The degree of collection necessary for a class depends upon the difficulties of the tests. In a class that calls for walk, trot, and canter both directions, a horse can travel in a medium frame (that is, with moderate collection) and perform quite well; but in a class that calls for further testing—such as counter canter, simple changes, or the like—the horse must be collected into a shorter frame to assure the rider's success in these tests of precision (Figs. 4-30A, B).

A.

B.

Figs. 4-29A, B—At the canter, the chestnut horse is leaning on its forehand and traveling "strung out" at both ends (A). In comparison, the black horse is cantering in a balanced "medium frame"—that is, moderately collected—with its forehand light (B). Photograph A by A. O. White, Jr./B by Suzie Richburg

A.

B.

Figs. 4-30A, B—Compare the horse moving in a "medium frame" (Fig. 4-29B) with the animal collected into a "short frame" for the counter canter (A). At the other extreme is a "long frame" which tends to allow a horse to travel on its forehand (B). Photographs by Suzie Richburg

Extension

"Extension" is the horse's lengthening from a medium stride into a long stride through increased impulsion. USET classes call for a "working trot rising showing a lengthening of stride," which is intended to test the rider's ability to create more impulsion in the horse and to control this extra thrust with a sensitive hand. Sensitivity of the hand is particularly important in this test, for a good rider can feel if the animal is about to go from the trot into the canter and will support the horse's front end with the hand, so the animal won't break into a canter sequence.

At the "strong posting trot"—as this lengthening of the stride is commonly called—the rider's upper body should be only a couple of degrees in front of the vertical, so the rider's weight, being behind the horse's motion, can act as a driving aid each time the rider sits (Fig. 4-31).

Fig. 4-31—During lengthening of the horse's stride at the posting trot, the rider's upper body should be only a few degrees in front of the vertical, so the weight of the torso can be used subtly as a driving aid. (Here, the rider's hands are a little too close to her body. She should move her elbows forward slightly and shorten her reins about 2 inches, maintaining the same frame of the horse, but allowing her hands to be in a more effective position.) Photograph by A. O. White, Jr.

However, the rider's weight should be used so subtly that you cannot see it forcing the horse forward; when the forcing is apparent, it is a fault called "pumping."

The strong trot is an appropriate test only for riders who are sophisticated enough to understand the relationship between collection and extension; a beginner will increase the animal's pace, rather than its impulsion, when asked to do a strong trot and will end up with a quick, medium-strided horse instead of a rhythmical, long-strided animal.

Severe Performance Faults

The worst performance faults in an equitation class are those which show that the rider is not in control—such as a horse that runs away with its rider (bolts) or stops at any point in the ring and refuses to go forward (balks or rears). If a horse's behavior appears to be a threat to its own rider or other competitors, you should excuse the rider from the ring.

Preferable to dangerous behavior, but still heavily penalized, are faults in which the rider does not perform the test. For instance, if you ask a rider to back his horse and the animal does not take even one step backward, or if you ask a rider to stop his horse and the animal moves around instead of standing immobile, you should severely penalize the rider for not performing the test.

Although not as bad as a "dangerous performance" or "not performing the test" at all, "breaking gait" is still a major error, because by momentarily switching to an incorrect gait, the rider does not perform the test in its entirety. When young or inexperienced riders commit this error, it usually is a downward break from the canter to the trot from lack of enough leg support; experienced riders are more likely to break gait upward from the trot into the canter during extension.

Quality of Performance

After weeding out competitors who commit "severe performance faults," compare the performances of the remaining riders. (Unless the class is terrible, the "severe performance faults" will keep those who committed them out of the ribbons.) You should pin the class by considering each rider's position as it relates to the quality of performance.

"Quality of performance" is not the quality of the horse as a hunter, but is what the rider is able to accomplish on his horse. In equitation classes, if one rider does an excellent job on a mediocre horse, he should pin above another rider who does a poor job on a wonderful horse, for you are judging the rider's capabilities alone.

This doesn't mean that the quality of the horse doesn't matter, for what the rider is able to accomplish often depends on the horse's ability. For instance, if a good rider gets on a rough-moving animal on the flat, the performance may look choppy when compared to that of other good riders on better movers. Although the rider need not have the fanciest hunter in the world to get a ribbon in equitation, he should choose a horse that does not have severe locomotion, conformation, or disposition problems which will continually put him at a disadvantage.

Tests on the Flat

Test 1— "Halt (4 to 6 seconds) and/or back." To properly perform the halt, the rider presses the horse forward with a supporting leg through the downward transition, so that the animal keeps its hocks engaged as it moves to the halt. By using a series of half-halts, the rider maintains lightness in the animal's forehand during the transition. The final picture at the halt should be of a horse standing squarely and on the bit, ready to respond to the rider's next request.

A very poor transition to the halt is marked by the horse pulling against the rider's hands and trailing its hocks behind—i.e., a horse that is "strung out." The horse may open its mouth in resistance, or may set its jaw and pull very hard. These errors result from the rider's hands being too strong in relation to his legs, which is an error in basic concept that should be heavily penalized. Even at the most elementary level, the rider must demonstrate the leg as the primary aid and the hand as a secondary, complementary aid. As the rider progresses to the point where collection of the horse is expected, he should not allow the hand to overpower the legs—an easy mistake to make when collection is first introduced.

The error of an overpowering hand may not be marked by such a severe reaction as a resistant, pulling horse. Instead, the horse may stay light on the bit, but "slam on the brakes" with its front feet and leave its quarters stringing out behind as it performs a downward transition to the halt. Again, the horse should move forward into the halt, so that when it reaches immobility, it is standing square, on the bit, and ready to react to the rider's next command.

Once the horse reaches the halt, it should stand quietly for several seconds, so there is no question about the animal's obedience. As the rider reaches the halt, he can square his horse's legs by pressing the horse forward, never by backing the animal. The reason for this is that the hocks should be engaged by forward thrust, not by moving the horse's body backwards to position it correctly over them. The rider should square the legs in the final step of the downward transition, rather than halting for a second or two, then moving forward a step, which would be considered an interruption in the required 4- to 6-second immobile stance.

The halt is a useful test, for it points out the balance of the rider's aids during the downward transition. This test can be used by itself, but it is frequently seen in conjunction with the test of backing.

Backing a horse correctly is an art. Just as fine dancers exude energy even while they stand upon a stage, a rider must also create this sense of energy in his horse as it stands poised to back. The readiness of the animal is caused by the rider's legs, which subtly signal the animal to anticipate movement. In conjunction with pressure from the legs, the hands keep a steady feel of the horse's mouth, so that if the animal begins to move forward, it will be restricted. Prior to the actual backing movement, then, the rider must use his legs to create this anticipation in the horse, yet be sensitive enough to feel whether the horse is going to stand or move about; he must be ready with a restricting hand in case the horse starts to move too soon.

Once the horse is alert and ready for motion, the rider adds more leg to encourage the horse forward onto the bit and increases his hand pressure to prevent the animal from stepping forward. Pressed into the restricting hand by the rider's leg, the horse, unable to move forward, begins to step backward. As the horse starts to go in reverse, the rider's leg and hand pressure ease up to reward the animal for moving backward. (The hand and leg should exert the minimal amount of pressure necessary to accomplish the required number of backward steps in a steady rhythm. If the rider is "overriding" his horse by using too much hand and leg, he should be penalized.) As soon as the backward steps are completed, the rider increases leg pressure and decreases hand pressure, so the horse moves forward. The animal should return to its original position in the same number of steps.

Requiring very good rider coordination and sensitivity to the horse's energy, backing is often poorly performed even at the highest level of equitation competition. Especially in classes of very young riders, you will see competitors pulling their horses backward, using a great deal of hand and very little leg—the opposite of what you are looking for in a good backing test.

A poor backing performance usually results from the rider's lack of coordination or lack of practice on the horse he is showing. From most to least serious, the performance faults associated with backing are: (1) the horse raising its head and/or opening its mouth and refusing to step backward; (2) taking one or more steps forward before it backs; (3) backing crookedly; (4) taking the incorrect number of steps backward (if you have specified the number of steps); (5) not backing with the feet stepping in diagonal pairs, but rather sliding backward in a sloppy fashion; and (6) being unwilling to go forward immediately following the backward steps.

Although these faults are listed from most serious to least serious in a general sense, their penalties would depend on the degree of disobedience in each specific case. For instance, a horse that drags its feet backward reluctantly, rather than stepping backward in diagonal pairs, is worse than a horse that hesitates slightly after backing before it moves forward into its original place. However, a horse that slides backward reluctantly would pin over a horse that not only hesitates to go forward after backing, but absolutely refuses to do so without being forced by its rider.

Performances that should be pinned high are those that demonstrate willing obedience of the horse as it starts to move forward onto the bit and, finding a restrictive hand, steps backward the correct number of steps as specified by the judge. This test should be flowing, so there is no hesitation between the backward motion and resumption of forward motion into the original position. The horse's head should remain low and its mouth closed, not gaping in resistance. Its feet should move in diagonal pairs in a steady rhythm; and once the proper number of steps has been completed, the horse should willingly go forward into its original position, returning in the same number of steps as it took going backward. From head to tail, the horse should remain straight and not resist by throwing its haunches to one side or the other.

Throughout the backing test, the rider's body must be erect—on the vertical—so that he stays with the horse's motion as it moves backward. His eyes should be looking straight ahead, not cast downward watching the horse as it performs the test (Fig. 4-32). The hand and leg aids should be so subtle that they are invisible to the judge. Any pulling or kicking by the rider is heavily penalized.

Fig. 4-32—This horse is backing correctly: stepping backward (rather than sliding the feet); moving the legs in diagonal pairs; remaining straight throughout the body; and keeping its mouth closed. (During this backing test without stirrups, the rider is holding her upper body slightly behind the vertical—rather than properly at the vertical—and her reins are a shade long.) Photograph by Suzie Richburg

Test 2—"Hand gallop." The "hand gallop" is distinguished from the "gallop" in that the hand gallop is less extended and is a three-beat gait, while the gallop, which calls for much greater pace and extension, causes each hoof to be placed separately and creates four beats. The "hand gallop" is so called because it is a "gallop in hand"; in other words, the rider restricts the horse's extension with his hands and prevents the animal from extending into a four-beat rhythm.

The hand gallop should be executed at 14 to 16 miles per hour; however, it is best judged as a pace greater than that of the normal canter, but not so great as to appear unsafe for the size of the ring in which the horse is showing. You must be careful not to ask for this test in rings that are very small or that have unsafe footing, for the small ring restricts the proper pace, and poor footing could cause an accident.

When individual testing is designated, the hand gallop (Test 2) is usually used in conjunction with the halt (Test 1). Prior to individual testing, instruct the riders to pick up a canter just before a specified corner, hand gallop their horses down the following long side of the ring, and halt just before the upcoming corner (Fig. 4-33). In this way, each rider can make an upward transition into the canter, assume two-point position, and increase his horse's pace around the corner, so the animal will be at the proper speed by the beginning of the long side.

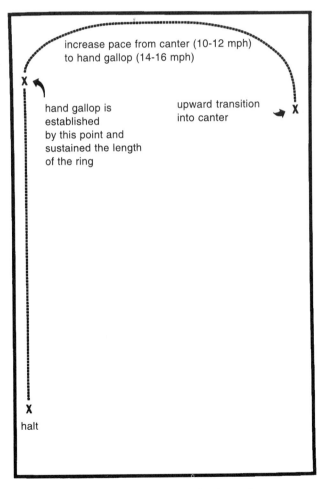

increase pace from canter (10-12 mph)
to hand gallop (14-16 mph)

X

hand gallop is
established
by this point and
sustained the length
of the ring

upward transition
into canter   X

X
halt

Fig. 4-33—Hand gallop and halt. Diagram by the author

In equitation classes, the halt should be performed without use of a pulley rein (the very powerful emergency rein aid in which the rider presses one hand on the horse's mane, just in front of the withers, and pulls back with the other hand to stop an uncontrollable horse). The ideal halt is prompt but smooth, with the horse keeping its hocks under its body, rather than throwing them out behind and "slamming on the brakes" in front. Once the horse has halted, it should stand immobile for several seconds before moving back into line with the other competitors.

Smoothness and control are important elements in this test. The rider performs the upward transition into the canter in "three-point position"—his legs and seat making three points of contact with the horse—while his upper body is inclined about 2 to 3 degrees in front of the vertical. Following the upward transition, the rider assumes two-point position—his two legs being in contact with the horse while his seat is held out of the saddle—and he inclines his upper body about 20 degrees in front of the vertical. The rider increases the pace to the proper speed along the corner and maintains this pace down the long side. To perform the halt, he sinks into three-point position during the downward transition, with his body returning to only a few degrees in front of the vertical. If the rider drops his upper body behind the vertical and hauls on the horse's mouth, he is severely penalized for roughness.

Test 2 can be used as a group test, but the number of horses galloping at one time should be limited for the sake of the competitors' safety and easy viewing by the judge. (Eight horses is the number allowed in the hunter division, and although it is not specified for the equitation division, it is a reasonable guideline). When asking for a group hand gallop, be sure not to let the test last too long. The chance of the horses misbehaving in a dangerous manner is greatly increased as the test is prolonged.

In group testing, scan the ring to see if each horse has reached the appropriate pace and, if you call for the halt, scan the ring again to check for fidgety animals unwilling to stand immobile. It will be impossible to see every horse's downward transition, but try to be aware of any riders having trouble with an uncooperative horse, especially those just shy of riding a runaway. As in all cases, lack of control is severely penalized.

Test 3—"Figure eight at trot, demonstrating change of diagonals. At left diagonal, rider should be sitting the saddle when left front leg is on the ground; at right diagonal, rider should be sitting the saddle when right front leg is on the ground; when circling clockwise at a trot, rider should be on left diagonal; when circling counter clockwise at a trot, rider should be on the right diagonal." The description of Test 3 emphasizes the importance of diagonals during the figure eight at the trot. Diagonals have this importance because they affect the horse's balance at this gait.

We are mainly concerned with the horse's *outside foreleg* at the trot because: (1) the *outside legs* reach farther than the inside legs when a horse is on a circle—because the outside legs are tracking a larger circle; and (2) the rider's upper body, inclined forward with the motion of the horse at the trot, can greatly affect the horse's *forehand*. If the rider lifts his weight as the horse's outside foreleg goes forward, he frees this leg to reach its maximum extension; and, if he sits when this leg hits the ground, he adds weight at the moment the horse is best able to handle it. Thus, by keeping the proper diagonal—rising when the outside foreleg goes forward and sitting when it is placed on the ground—the rider is aiding the animal in keeping its balance around curves at the trot.

In judging this test, note the shape of the figure the horse is making. Riders often make the mistake of performing the figure eight as the number eight is written, with diagonal lines connecting two arcs (Fig. 4-34A). The correct figure is composed of two adjoining circles of equal size, with a small straight segment along the center line at which the circles join—which is where the horse straightens its body for a few steps in order to gradually change its bend from one direction to the other (Fig. 4-34B).

Riding two circles of equal size requires thinking ahead. An intelligent competitor will map out his path beforehand, so you should allow a little planning time before the test for those with the foresight to use it. It is best if, before judging this test, you designate the *center line*, along which the horse should approach the figure, by standing on that line. The rider can then choose his *center point*: the exact place at which the transitions will occur. (The rider should plan to emphasize the center point by sitting the trot down the center line and posting as he starts his figure at the center point. Although going from the walk or halt into the posting trot could also designate the center point, changing from the sitting trot to the posting trot is the smoothest means of designation. The rider must signal the end of the test by halting at the center point.)

Once the rider has planned where his center point will be, he should map out a path for the first circle and then the second, looking for stationary reference points (preferably one for each quadrant of each circle) to help him stay on his path. If he sees that he will be unable to keep the

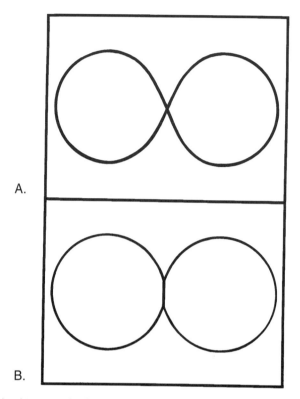

A.

B.

Figs. 4-34A, B—The figure eight is performed incorrectly if the rider crosses the center point on diagonal lines (A). When performing this figure correctly, the rider straightens his horse for a few steps on the center line before changing the animal's bend toward the direction of travel (B). Diagrams by the author

second circle the same size as the first—a jump is in the way, for instance—he should go back and plan another path that will allow the circles to be of equal size.

While performing the test, the rider should keep his reference points in mind and concentrate on going from one to the next, demonstrating impulsion, bending, the proper frame for the test, and the correct diagonals. As you watch the test, you'll see which riders have planned their routes, for lack of forethought will result in mistakes such as a near collision with an object in the ring, the formation of ovals instead of circles, or one circle being larger than the other. The more obvious the lack of planning, the heavier the penalty you assess.

From most to least severe, the faults you will often see in Test 3 are: (1) wrong diagonals; (2) an imprecise figure—such as the figure performed as the number eight is written, the circles being unequal in size, ovals being performed instead of circles, or the rider missing the center point; (3) lack of bending; and (4) a rhythm that is too dull or too quick, lacking in steady impulsion.

Test 4—"Figure eight at canter on correct lead, demonstrating simple change of lead. This is a change whereby the horse is brought back into a walk or trot and re-started into a canter on the opposite lead. Figures to be commenced in center of two circles so that one change of lead is shown." In Test 4, emphasis is placed on the proper leads at the canter and the correct changing of leads. Although the change may occur through either the walk or the trot, the walk is traditionally correct and, being considered greater in difficulty, should receive slightly higher marks if the performances are executed with equal accuracy and smoothness.

The shape of the figure eight is the same at the canter as at the trot—two adjoining circles of equal size. During the lead change, a horse should take only a few trotting or walking steps. The ideal is two steps (in either gait) during the change, which is the most prompt change possible; but if the horse needs more steps to balance itself in order to change leads smoothly, the rider can allow it to take four or six steps between leads. (The steps must be in multiples of two for the horse to have the proper sequence of feet to pick up the new lead. Six steps are the outside limit and should be used only for young horses which take that long to get their balance; older horses should be better trained, using only two or four steps during the change.)

As in the figure eight at the trot, the rider plans his test and marks the beginning and end of it clearly for the judge by picking up the canter from the sitting trot (or from the walk or halt) to designate the beginning of the figure, and by halting at the center point to mark completion of the test. For the changing of leads, the horse should pick up the new lead as the rider's shoulder is over the center point of the figure. This means that all walking or trotting steps should occur before the horse reaches the center point, so the rider must anticipate how many steps his horse will need between leads and perform a downward transition the necessary distance from the center point.

The most heavily penalized faults in a figure eight test at the canter are, from most to least serious: (1) incorrect leads; (2) an imprecise figure; (3) lack of bending; (4) a rhythm that is too dull (so the horse canters in four beats instead of three) or a rhythm that is too quick; and (5) a late change, in which the rider misfigures the number of steps his horse will need to take between the leads and crosses the center point still walking or trotting.

Test 5—"Work collectively at walk, trot, or canter." This test has already been discussed in depth in the sections on Position and Performance.

Test 6—"Pull up and halt (4 to 6 seconds)." Test 6 is actually the same as Test 1, for it is impossible to halt without having pulled up first (that is, having performed a downward transition). Consequently, you can refer to Test 1 for the explanation of Test 6.

Test 8—"Ride without stirrups or drop and pick up stirrups." Evidently, these two tests were put together not because they were considered to be of equal difficulty, but because they both deal with stirrups. First, examine the easier of the two: dropping and picking up the stirrups. It is a suitable test for a group of young riders, for they are likely to lose their stirrups at one time or another and should be able to get them back without having to bend down to locate them.

Dropping and picking up the stirrups, whether it is asked of the competitor while moving or stationary, involves using feeling, rather than vision; thus, the test is properly executed with the rider looking forward the entire time. Dropping both feet out of his stirrups, the rider can tell where the irons are by feeling where they hit in relation to his ankle bones. With this knowledge, he can insert his feet into the irons without dropping his eyes to look.

As for the much more difficult task of riding without stirrups, you are looking for riders who show no change in position when their stirrups are removed, but who appear as stable and effective as they did with their irons. Competitors should appear well-balanced in their upper bodies and not depend upon reins for balance when the stirrups are missing. The leg must be in the same position as with stirrups, with the ankle retaining its angular appearance. There should be no wiggling of the leg at the trot or swinging of the leg at the canter that could cause the horse's performance to be adversely affected.

When calling for any tests without stirrups, allow the riders sufficient time to cross the stirrup leathers so the irons won't bounce against the horses' sides.

Test 10—"Dismount and mount. Individually." Test 10 is used to determine if the rider can mount by himself without pulling on the horse's mouth or poking the animal in the side with the toe of the boot. This is an elementary test appropriate for young riders, as long as the riders are not so small in relation to their mounts that they cannot possibly mount from the ground. Consider the riders' sizes in relation to their animals before calling for this test, or else you may end up giving a competitor a leg up before it's all over.

Test 10 can also be used for older age groups, but it is rather elementary for their capabilities. Although it can be distressing to competitors who mount by way of their grooms and who have not had to mount from the ground in years, even those riders generally know how to get on properly and will come through in the pinch of competition. Therefore, Test 10 is not the best means of separating the good from the bad in older age groups.

To dismount, the rider puts both reins in his left hand—along with a clump of mane that will keep him from inadvertently pulling on the horse's mouth during the dismount and will assure fixed rein pressure, preventing the horse from walking forward as the rider is getting off. The rider can dismount in either of two ways: by dropping the outside stirrup and swinging the outside leg over the croup to the near side, then dropping the near stirrup and sliding down the horse's side, or by dropping both feet out of the stirrups and vaulting to the ground on the near side. Either way is acceptable.

Landing on the ground facing the horse's near side (at which point the test of dismounting is completed), the rider then turns to face the horse's rear end, still holding the reins and mane in the left hand. Grasping the back of the stirrup iron with his right hand and turning it toward himself, the rider inserts his left foot in the iron and turns the toe of his boot into the girth, so it won't press into the horse's flesh as he mounts (Fig. 4-35). The rider's right hand is then free to grasp the cantle of the saddle and, aided by one or two bounces on his right foot, the rider can pull himself up above the saddle and swing his right leg over the horse. He should not land heavily on the horse's back, but should gradually sink into the saddle and separate his reins into the proper position for riding while finding the stirrup iron by feel, rather than looking for it or reaching down to position it on the foot. (In order to separate dismounting from mounting more distinctly, the rider may move to the front of his horse following the dismount and stand facing the same direction as his horse, then turn and begin the mounting process. This

Fig. 4-35—When mounting properly, the rider holds the reins taut enough that the horse won't walk forward; grasps the mane to prevent pulling on the animal's mouth when mounting; and turns the toe of the boot into the girth, rather than pressing it into the horse's flesh. Photograph by A. O. White, Jr.

break between mounting and dismounting is not mandatory, however, for once the rider's feet have touched the ground, the dismounting phase has ended and the mounting phase can immediately begin.)

Test 11—"Turn on the forehand." The turn on the forehand is a schooling exercise executed from the halt and is employed to teach the horse obedience. The hindquarters of the horse should move in regular, quiet steps in a circle around its forehand. This movement may be executed through 90, 180, or 360 degrees.

The turn on the forehand can be performed in either of two ways: the horse moving away from the direction it is bent (basic) or the horse moving into the direction it is bent (advanced). A competitor is correct whether he bends his horse outward or inward; but whichever way he chooses, he must stick to that method throughout the turn and not let the bend of the horse slip from one direction to the other.

If a railing were on the horse's right side, the animal would have to move its haunches to the left to complete a 180-degree turn ("half-turn") on the forehand (Figs. 4-36A, B). The horse's neck in the basic turn is bent slightly toward the rail with a right indirect rein. The rider's right leg is drawn back about 4 inches behind the normal left-leg position in order to activate the haunches into sideways movement, and because of this leg position, the horse's body will remain basically straight from withers to tail, rather than being bent around the rider's right leg. However, the bending in the horse's neck and the motion of the animal's legs during the turn will make the horse appear slightly bent from head to tail. (Figure 4-36A reflects this bent appearance in the body of the middle, "moving" horse, while the first horse has only its neck slightly bent as it is positioned to begin the turn, and the last position shows the horse straight from head to tail as the rider straightens the animal in the final step of the turn.)

While the rider's right hand maintains the bend in the neck and his right leg pushes the haunches to the left, his left hand and leg restrict the horse from stepping forward or backward, or moving hurriedly to the left. The horse's steps should be cadenced, with the right foreleg stepping in place (not stuck to the ground and twisting), the left foreleg stepping around the right foreleg, and the right hind leg crossing the left hind leg. It usually takes four steps to make a half-turn on the forehand on a willing horse, but the number will vary somewhat according to each animal. Therefore, don't be concerned with the specific number of steps as much as with the maintenance of a steady rhythm throughout the test and with the successful completion of the turn.

For the more advanced turn on the forehand, the horse's neck will be slightly bent to the left as the animal stands with the railing on its right side (Fig. 4-36B). The rider uses a left indirect rein, but his legs are positioned the same as above, with the right leg slightly back and the left leg in normal position. The rider presses with his right leg, and the horse's body bends slightly around the rider's left leg as the animal moves to the left—into the bend. The horse's feet step in the pattern described above. This method of turning on the forehand is more difficult than the first because it requires the horse to move into, instead of away from, the direction it is bent.

At the intermediate stage of riding, the emphasis is on making the horse supple through movements such as leg-yielding and shoulder-in, both of which require the horse to move away from the direction it is

Turn on the Forehand—Basic

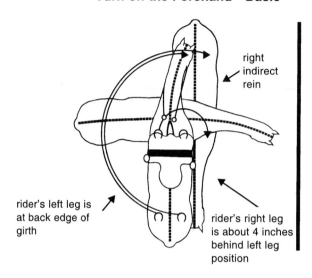

right
indirect
rein

rider's left leg is
at back edge of
girth

rider's right leg
is about 4 inches
behind left leg
position

Turn on the Forehand—Advanced

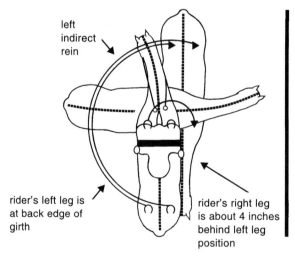

left
indirect
rein

rider's left leg is
at back edge of
girth

rider's right leg
is about 4 inches
behind left leg
position

Figs. 4-36A, B—In the basic turn on the forehand, the horse is bent away from the direction of travel (A). In the advanced turn on the forehand, the horse moves toward the bend (B). The diagrams show the aids of the rider and movement of the horse's legs during the basic and advanced turns. Diagrams by the author

bent (although in the leg-yield, the horse is only slightly bent in its poll; while in the shoulder-in, the horse is bent from head to tail). In advanced riding, however, we expect greater control over the horse, so the animal will not only willingly move away from leg pressure, but also will be obedient enough to remain bent when asked to move toward the direction in which it is bent. Movements such as the advanced turn on the forehand, turn on the haunches, half-pass (two track), travers (haunches in), renvers (haunches out), and pirouette are tests of the horse's obedience and the rider's ability to keep his horse balanced when it is moving toward the direction in which it is bent. When performing each of those movements correctly, the horse will remain bent in the direction of travel throughout the test and keep a steady and impulsive rhythm, staying solidly on the bit. I will not go into the specifics of most of the movements mentioned above, since they are not required in the show ring, but will discuss the advanced turn on the forehand (Test 11) and the turn on the haunches (Test 17).

A rider who is knowledgeable and coordinated enough to do the advanced turn on the forehand should be given credit for his sophistication. Even though we speak of these turns as "basic" and "advanced," the turn on the forehand in either form should be reserved for more experienced riders in the fourteen- to seventeen-year age group, for younger riders rarely understand this test.

Although I have explained at length the difference between the basic and advanced turns, the most important aspect of the turn on the forehand is not the direction in which the horse is bent, but how willingly the horse moves from the rider's leg. Ranked from most to least serious, performance faults frequently committed during a turn on the forehand are: (1) the horse backing, rather than moving sideways—a fault akin to other serious faults involving evasion behind the rider's leg; (2) the animal moving sideways for a step or two, then halting and refusing to complete the test until the rider forces it to do so; (3) the horse walking forward a step before submitting laterally to the rider's leg; (4) the horse changing its bend during the exercise from the original direction in which it was bent; and (5) the animal grinding its pivotal foreleg into the ground, rather than stepping in the rhythm of the walk. Although a horse should not walk forward as an evasion of the rider's aids during this test, the pivotal forefoot may move slightly during the turn so the horse is tracking a small half-circle with the pivotal foot, rather than stepping in place. There is no rule as to the size of this half-circle, but generally speaking, a turn in which the pivotal foot remains within a 9-inch radius is acceptable.

Throughout the turn on the forehand, the horse's neck should remain in a steady, slightly flexed position, and the judge should penalize a horse that shows resistance to the rider's aids by raising or lowering its head or by pulling on or dropping behind the bit. The penalty for these disobediences is determined by the accompanying errors, since all are related to the horse's unwillingness to obey the rider's leg—an unwillingness that begins in the haunches.

For the turn on the forehand performed in the opposite direction, the pivotal foot would be the left foreleg and the rider's aids would be reversed.

Test 12—"Figure eight at canter on correct lead demonstrating flying change of lead." For a flying change, the rider asks his horse to switch leads at the completion of the first circle of the figure eight without breaking into either the walk or the trot. The initial circle is usually performed to the right; but if a horse is better at switching from the left to the right lead, then the rider can make the decision to start with a circle to the left and not be penalized, provided you do not specify otherwise in your instructions.

When a rider performs the test starting with a circle to the right, on approaching the end of this circle, he begins to even out his hand and leg positions to straighten the animal and uses a series of half-halts to "set up" the horse for the change. Keeping the animal from leaning toward the upcoming direction of travel—by using a supporting left leg and left bearing rein—and drawing the right leg back about 4 inches behind the girth as the horse reaches the center point of the figure, the rider signals the horse to change leads with pressure from his right leg and sensitively controls the horse's forward movement with his hands, so the horse doesn't run from the leg aid.

To do a flying change, the horse must be well-balanced, not drifting toward the outside of the first circle, since this would thrust excess weight onto the side of the horse which must be light for the change. As the horse switches leads, it should not fall into the new direction, but should lift its front end slightly and switch in one motion of the front and hind limbs—the horse landing on the new lead all at once. Just after the switch, the rider must bend his horse in the new direction of travel, so the animal will be balanced around the circle.

Performance faults seen during the figure eight with a flying change of lead, from most to least serious, are: (1) the rider not getting his horse to switch to the new lead and allowing the animal to counter-canter or cross-canter the entire second circle; (2) the rider allowing the horse to remain on the original lead past the center point, so the horse counter-canters a portion of the second circle before switching to the new lead; (3) the rider getting his horse to switch partially at the center point, so the horse cross-canters a few steps before changing entirely to the new lead; and (4) the rider allowing his horse to speed up during the switch or letting the horse bounce a few steps leading into the change.

The figure eight with a flying change is a difficult test that should be reserved for advanced equitation riders.

Test 13—"Execute serpentine at a trot and/or canter on correct lead demonstrating simple or flying changes of lead." This is another test of the rider's understanding of diagonals and leads, involving more changes than required in the figure eight tests.

When you call for a serpentine, specify the gait or gaits, type of lead changes (if applicable), and number of loops—generally three or four loops (Fig. 4-37). The loops begin and end as the rider's shoulder crosses the center line. A serpentine commences at one end of a center line (chosen by the competitor or designated by the judge) and ends at the other end of that line, with the loops on each side of the center line being equal in proportion.

To start the test, the rider sits the trot to the point at which the serpentine is to begin. He then designates the center line by posting on the correct diagonal, if the test is performed at the trot, or picking up the proper lead, if the test is performed at the canter. He bends his horse in the direction of travel around the loops and straightens the animal for a few steps as it approaches, crosses, and departs the center line. The rider's shoulder should be directly above the center line when he halts to mark completion of the serpentine. (If you ask for two serpentines—one at the trot and one at the canter—the rider should not halt after the first, but should go directly into the canter from the trot, by sitting the trot for a few steps before the center line and picking up the canter as his shoulder passes over the center line.)

If you ask for simple changes, the walking or trotting steps should occur prior to the center line, so the horse can pick up the new lead as the rider's shoulder crosses the center line. Flying changes also occur as the rider's shoulder crosses the center line.

Faults that can be committed during the serpentine are, from most to least serious: (1) performing the incorrect number of loops; (2) not getting the correct diagonals at the trot or correct leads at the canter; (3) not

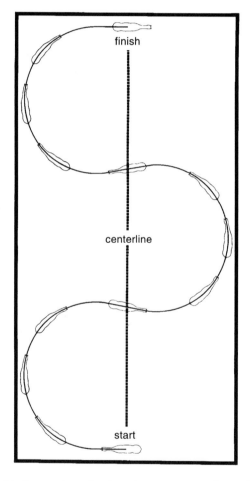

Fig. 4-37—A bird's-eye view of a three-loop serpentine shows the horse correctly bent in the direction of travel on the loops and straight in the body as it crosses the center line. Diagram by the author

having the horse bent in the direction of travel around the loops; (4) overshooting the center line during the change of diagonals or leads or at the beginning or end of the test; and (5) rough transitions or lead changes.

The serpentine is an appropriate test for all levels beyond the absolute beginner. It can be a simple test for a young rider (for example, performing a three-loop serpentine at the posting trot) or an advanced test for a sophisticated rider (such as, performing a four-loop serpentine demonstrating flying changes of lead). Consider the competitors' level of ability as a group and choose the appropriate test.

Test 14—"Change leads on a line demonstrating a simple or flying change of lead." Precision, straightness, and willing submission of the horse are your main concerns in judging Test 14. It is best if you designate the line by standing at the end of it, so you can watch each competitor head-on as he or she performs the test. You must also specify whether the riders are to perform simple or flying changes; but if you call for simple changes, each rider makes his own decision as to the use of the walk or trot.

In judging all tests of precision, you mark higher those performances that show forethought—ones in which you see the competitor has marked off mentally the places where he should make the changes you are requiring. For instance, if you ask for two simple changes, the competitor should mentally divide the ring into three equal sections down the line, noting stationary objects in or around the ring that will help him mark each section (Fig. 4-38). Beginning the test at the far end of the ring, facing you, he can pick up the first lead, make a simple change at his first marker, take the second lead, make the second simple change at his second marker, and pick up the third and final lead before halting in front of you.

For the simple changes, the trotting or walking steps should occur prior to the rider's mental marker, so he can perform the upward transition as his shoulder is directly above the marker. Flying changes also should occur as the rider's shoulder crosses the marker.

It doesn't matter which lead the horse begins on—unless you have specified the initial lead in your instructions. When this test is used as a flat test alone, the rider begins with an upward transition into the canter at the beginning of the line to mark the start of the test. If the test is used in conjunction with jumping tests, however, the rider should complete the last fence, collect his horse, and turn down the line without making a downward transition (or flying change) until the first marker for the changing of leads.

Faults you may see in this test, from most to least severe, are: (1) overshooting the points at which the leads should be changed—which indicates either lack of planning or lack of control; (2) drifting off the

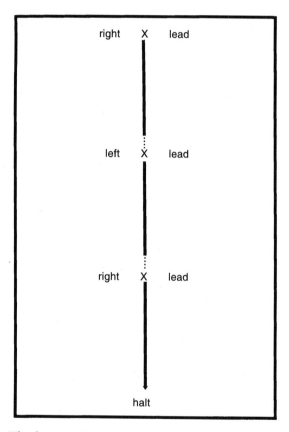

Fig. 4-38—The diagram shows the division of a line for "two simple changes"—that is, three leads. It doesn't matter which lead the rider starts on, but he must alternate leads down the line, never picking up the same lead in succession. X marks the initial upward transition into the canter and the points at which the leads are changed. The dotted lines designate where transitions occur during simple changes through the walk or sitting trot. The rider should mark completion of the test by halting while still on the line. Diagram by the author

center line, which shows the rider is not using his hands and legs to limit the animal's lateral movement properly; and (3) making rough transitions during the simple changes, or a rough switching of leads in the flying changes.

Of course, if a rider overshoots his designated points for lead changes so far that the horse performs only part of the test—if it runs out of room before picking up the final lead, for example—he deserves the heaviest penalty, since he has not performed the given test.

Test 15—"Change horses. (Note: this test is the equivalent of two tests.)" When you ask riders to change horses for further flat testing, be sure one rider will not be at a disadvantage due to the build of the horse he or she is asked to ride. For instance, if you ask a girl of medium height, whose horse has a medium build, to switch with a tall boy on a very large animal, the girl will have the advantage because she can still look nice on the large horse, while the boy will look ridiculous on a horse too small for him. To do justice to the competitors, try to switch them onto horses that suit their builds, so the awful picture of a mismatched horse-rider combination will not get in the way of judging each rider's position and quality of performance.

The test of switching a rider onto a strange horse is used to determine the rider's ability to cope with an animal at the spur of the moment, without the benefit of practice time. If one rider is attempting to deal with a strange horse in the proper way, but must be a little rough to achieve results, he should place above another rider who is afraid to assert himself on an unfamiliar animal and looks as if he is trying to survive rather than compete. However, if a third rider gets the proper results using invisible aids, he should be placed above the other two; for, ideally, you are looking for a rider as relaxed and effective on a strange horse as he was on his own.

Test 16—"Canter on counter lead. (Note: no more than twelve horses may counter canter at one time.)" Test 16 is used to determine an advanced rider's degree of coordination and sensitivity and his ability to maintain obedience in his horse.

The counter canter calls for the horse to take the outside lead, rather than the inside one it normally uses to maintain its balance on corners. While traveling counterclockwise, the horse would be on the right lead for the counter canter; while moving clockwise, it would be on the left lead.

The rider's position is extremely important in maintaining the counter lead. To take the right lead while moving in a counterclockwise direction, the rider should have his left leg about a hand's breadth behind the back edge of the girth to give the aid for the canter depart, to maintain impulsion, and to keep the horse's haunches from swinging left. He should put his right leg just behind the back edge of the girth—to keep the horse's body bent to the right—and position his hands in a right indirect rein so that the horse's neck is properly bent, that is, slightly toward the leading right front leg (Fig. 4-39A).

The rider's right hand and leg work together to keep the horse bent to the right, while the left hand (used as a slight bearing rein against the horse's neck) and left leg work together to prevent the animal from leaning toward the inside of the ring and switching leads. The rider's upper body is positioned on the vertical throughout the test, so his weight can act in conjunction with his left leg to drive the horse forward, preventing it from four-beating, breaking gait, or switching leads. However, you should penalize the rider if he noticeably presses the horse forward with his seat, for his leg aid should be predominant. To perform the counter canter in the other direction, the rider reverses his aids (Fig. 4-39B).

Do not prolong this test, for it is difficult in itself, and the problem of horses trying to pass each other while on the counter lead makes it even harder. When watching the counter canter, notice any animals that are strung out, for they are the most likely to switch leads; and, if they do, you shouldn't miss it.

Faults you may see in Test 16 are, from most to least severe: (1) the rider never getting the horse on the counter lead; (2) allowing the horse to break gait or switch leads; (3) letting the horse travel strung out on its forehand, or letting the horse four-beat the canter from lack of impulsion; and (4) bending the horse toward the inside—instead of the outside—of the ring.

Test 17—"Turn on the haunches from the walk." The *AHSA Rule Book* describes the turn on the haunches as follows: "The horse's forehand moves in even, quiet and regular steps around the horse's inner hindleg while maintaining the rhythm of the walk. In the half turn on the haunches, the horse is not required to step with its inside hind leg in the same spot each time it leaves the ground, but may move slightly forward. Backing or loss of rhythm are considered a serious fault. This movement may be executed through 90 degrees, 180 degrees, or 360 degrees."

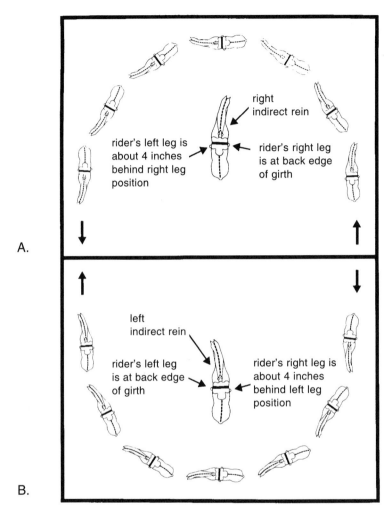

A.

B.

Figs. 4-39A, B—A bird's-eye view of the counter canter shows the rider's aids and the direction of the horse's bend for counterclockwise (A) and clockwise (B) movement. The horse should be bent from head to tail slightly toward the outside (leading) foreleg on the ends of the ring. (Theoretically, the horse is no longer on the "counter lead" on the long sides of the arena because the horse is equally balanced on either lead when traveling on a straight line. However, the horse must maintain the outside lead both on the ends and long sides of the ring during this test.) The horse's body should become straighter on the long sides of the ring, so there is only a hint of bending to the outside. Diagrams by the author

Just as the advanced method of performing the turn on the forehand requires the horse to move into the bend, so does the turn on the haunches. If the horse is walking with the railing on its right side, it will have to pivot to the left to complete a 180-degree turn ("half-turn") on the haunches (Fig. 4-40).

First, the rider bends the horse's neck slightly away from the rail with a left indirect rein placed farther to the left than normal indirect rein position, so the left rein can act as a subtle leading (opening) rein while the right rein restricts forward movement and can be used as a bearing (neck) rein if necessary. Then, exerting pressure with his right leg—placed about a hand's breadth behind the position of the left leg—the rider displaces the horse to the left, causing its right foreleg to cross its left foreleg and its right hind leg to cross its left hind leg in the rhythm of the walk.

Ideally, the left hind leg would march in place, so that as the horse turned, its left hind foot would turn and step on its previous footprint. However, maintenance of enough impulsion to keep the hind feet marching in the rhythm of the walk, with the pivotal foot landing on the same spot each step, is nearly impossible. Therefore, it is acceptable for the pivotal foot (in this case, the left hind leg) to move slightly with each step, so the walk rhythm will be maintained by the pivotal foot making a small half-circle rather than stepping in place. The smaller this half-circle the better, and, as a rule of thumb, the radius of the turn made by the pivotal foot must not exceed 9 inches.

While moving during the turn on the haunches, the horse should remain bent from head to tail in the direction of travel, for the combination of the rider's right leg (placed 4 inches behind the girth) pushing the horse toward the rider's left leg (placed at the back edge of the girth) causes the horse to be wrapped around the rider's left leg—that is, bent from head to tail—as the animal steps around the turn. (Fig. 4-40 shows the bend from head to tail in the middle [moving] horse; while the initial position shows a horse only bent slightly in its neck—as the rider prepares it for the first step of the turn—and the final position shows a straight animal as the rider straightens the horse during the last step of the turn.) For the turn on the haunches in the opposite direction, the pivotal foot would be the right hind leg and the rider's aids would be reversed.

Faults that can be committed during the turn on the haunches, from most to least severe, are: (1) the horse backing, rather than moving side-

Turn on the Haunches

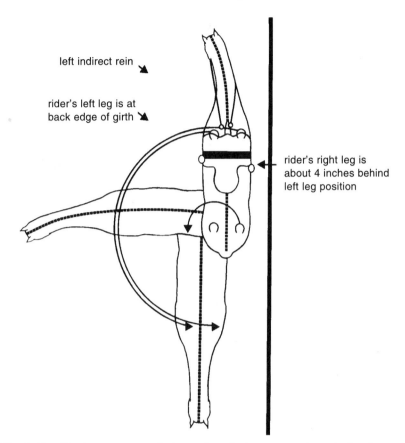

left indirect rein

rider's left leg is at
back edge of girth

rider's right leg is
about 4 inches behind
left leg position

Fig. 4-40—During a turn on the haunches, the horse moves into the bend.
The diagram shows the aids of the rider and movement of the horse's legs
during the turn on the haunches moving counterclockwise. For clockwise
movement, the aids are reversed. Diagram by the author

ways; (2) not remaining bent in the direction of travel; (3) halting for a
second or two between steps before finishing the test; and (4) walking
forward for a step.

In this test, notice that more emphasis is placed on the horse remaining bent toward the direction of travel than in the description of the
turn on the forehand. This is because in the turn on the forehand—a
basic exercise—emphasis is placed on the horse's willingness to move

from the rider's leg, with the bending (which can be in either direction) having secondary importance; the turn on the haunches, however, is an advanced exercise, and the only way it can be performed correctly is for the horse to move into the bend.

Although I have used a railing in the description of both the turn on the forehand and haunches, both tests can be asked of riders without any railing present.

Test 18—"Demonstration ride of approximately one minute. Rider must advise judge beforehand what ride he plans to demonstrate." Test 18 allows a rider to demonstrate the level of his skill by making up his own test. Since it takes time to plan a series of movements on the flat that best show one's abilities, it is advisable for the competitor to have worked out his plan prior to the horse show and committed at least one plan (if not several alternate ones also) to memory. The rider should attempt movements that best display his education and skill and not attempt movements so difficult for his level of riding that he is likely to make major faults. (Movements are not limited to other tests in Tests 1–18 but may also include schooling movements, such as shoulder-in, two-track, extended trot, etc.)

Test 18 is a wonderful test that should be used more often. It allows riders of outstanding ability to show their skills to the fullest, while it enables less talented riders in the same class to choose movements within their limitations. Test 18 is interesting for spectators and judges to watch and for competitors to perform because it allows more individuality than any of the other tests.

5

EQUITATION OVER FENCES

POSITION OVER FENCES

General Observations

In judging equitation classes over fences, as in classes on the flat, begin by focusing on the position of the rider's lower leg. You are looking for riders whose deep ankles reflect the downward distribution of their weight and whose lower legs stay fixed on their horses' sides at all times, between fences and in the air (Figs. 5-1A, B).

In the area of the thighs and buttocks, your emphasis is on the rider's ability to use two-point and three-point position appropriately. Two-point position, commonly called "galloping position," is used for a variety of purposes: racing, hunting, galloping cross-country, and showing in hunter or equitation classes over fences. The term "two-point position" means that only the rider's two legs are in contact with the horse, for his seat is held out of the saddle to free the animal's back (see Fig. 5-1A). When using two-point position between fences in hunter or equitation classes, the rider should incline his upper body approximately 20 degrees in front of the vertical, so he will be with the motion of the horse. (When two-point is used for competition involving greater speed—such as flat racing—the rider's upper body is inclined more forward to match the change in the horse's center of gravity.)

A.

B.

Figs. 5-1A, B—The rider's leg is securely fixed on her horse's side and weight is pressed into her heel both on the approach to the obstacle (A) and in the air (B). (In both photos, her seat is too far out of the saddle, causing her hands to be held high and her upper body to be slightly ahead of the horse's motion.) Photographs by Pennington Galleries

Three-point position—involving the rider's two legs and his seat—offers greater security than two-point and allows the rider's aids to be used more strongly (Fig. 5-2). Three-point position is used in jumper classes that require tight turns and equitation classes that have simulated jumper courses—such as the USET class and some Medal and Maclay classes. In "extreme three-point" position, the rider fixes his seat bones

Fig. 5-2—Firmly fixed on his horse's back in three-point position, the rider has maximum control of his animal. Although his set jaw draws his neck and shoulders slightly in front of the vertical, his seat and legs are so secure that he is undoubtedly master of his mount. Photograph by Pennington Galleries

firmly in the saddle and keeps his upper body on the vertical, giving himself maximum control of his horse. Since this position tends to rob the round of fluidity and subtlety, riders should use it only if absolutely necessary—that is, if a rider realizes that without the use of this position, he will not be able to negotiate a particularly tight turn with precision.

Preferable to the "extreme three-point" position, in which the rider's upper body is vertical and seat is fixed in the saddle, is a "modified three-point" position, in which the rider sinks his crotch into the saddle for the third point of contact and inclines his body halfway between two-point angulation and the vertical—that is, about 10 degrees in front of the vertical (Fig. 5-3). In modified three-point, the rider places some weight on his horse's back, but he is better able to lighten the animal's front end than when he is in two-point position, so he can ride trappy courses with precision. Although equitation courses never demand "extreme" or

Fig. 5-3—This rider merges the attributes of two-point and three-point position in a "modified three-point" seat. The 10-degree inclination of his upper body allows more freedom of the horse's back than does "extreme three-point" position, while the sinking of his crotch into the saddle offers him greater control than with "two-point position." Photograph by Pennington Galleries

"modified" three-point throughout, these positions can be useful to the rider in negotiating a tricky turn or an unusually short distance between fences.

No matter what degree of inclination the upper body has, the rider's back should stay straight from the base of the spine to the back of the rider's head, and should not show evidence of any of the upper-body errors previously discussed: loose back, roached back, swayback, rounded or forced-back shoulders, stretched-forward neck, set jaw, or cocked head.

The rider's arms and back should work together, with the back supporting the arms' restraining efforts during half-halts. Otherwise, the rider may be dislodged if the horse pulls between fences (Figs. 5-4A, B).

Approaching the Fence and in the Air

Legs Too Far Forward

A rider whose leg position is insecure during the approach to a fence will have difficulty staying with the motion of his horse as it jumps. At takeoff, his legs will not be able to give his upper body support and his torso may fall back, causing his legs to shoot forward. This combination of a forward leg position and the upper body behind the horse's motion in the air is called "getting left" (Fig. 5-5). You should penalize this fault very heavily, for it is the most serious airborne mistake a rider can make. It radically affects the horse's balance and causes abuse to the animal's back and (usually) its mouth as the rider falls backward in the air. A rider who manages to grab the mane and keep himself from "catching his horse in the mouth" redeems his performance a little; but getting left in any degree is a serious fault, for when a horse jumps, the rider must go with it, for his own and the animal's safety.

An insecure leg position is not the only cause of getting left, for on occasion a rider with a secure leg will make this error when his horse leaves the ground earlier than expected. More often, though, the riders you'll see getting left are beginners who have not yet developed either a sound leg position or a good eye for finding a distance to a fence.

Another fault that may appear with a forward leg position—both on the approach to and in the air over a fence—is a roached back. A rider whose leg is thrust forward may hover over his horse's front end in an effort to counterbalance his upper body against his leg. This "jackknifed" position indicates an ineffectual leg and back, as well as a lack of balance and security, and should be heavily penalized (Fig. 5-6).

A.

B.

Figs. 5-4A, B—Although the horse is resisting in Figure A—as indicated by its open mouth—the rider is properly using her back to reinforce her hands and arms in the half-halt, so she remains in control of the animal. In Figure B, the back is not reinforcing the hands, which are low and ineffective, and the rider is no longer in control. Photographs by Pennington Galleries

Fig. 5-5—By "getting left," this rider is drastically behind the horse's motion; her upper-body weight is pulling the horse out of its arc in the air. Photograph by Pennington Galleries

If a rider with a forward leg position doesn't counterbalance himself by inclining his upper body above his leg, he may keep his upper body behind the horse's motion on the approach to the fence, then throw his torso forward in the air, to catch up to his horse's motion. As the rider pivots on his knee to move from behind the motion to in front of the motion, his leg is too far forward on the approach to the fence and too far back in the air (Figs. 5-7A, B). The worst result of this radical upper body movement—commonly called "jumping up on the horse's neck"—is the unbalancing effect the rider's weight has on the horse by suddenly shifting forward just as the horse leaves the ground and becomes airborne.

Although you should give a major penalty for jumping up on the neck in an equitation class, the jackknifed position mentioned previously deserves an even heavier penalty, for three reasons. First, the rider whose upper body is vertical as he approaches the fence can use his arms and back to lift his horse's front end, lightening the forehand through the use of half-halts and enabling the animal to jump with greater ease. In comparison, the rider who hovers over his horse's neck increases the weight on its forehand and makes it more difficult for the animal to jump.

Fig. 5-6—The lack of weight in this rider's heel has allowed his lower leg to shoot forward. By counterbalancing his forward leg with a roached back, he assumes a "jackknifed" position. Photograph by Pennington Galleries

Second, the rider who sits vertically can place his horse at a good takeoff spot, either by using his seat as a driving aid, if the horse needs to extend to leave the ground at the proper place, or by using his arms and back as restraining aids, if the animal's stride needs shortening. Although the combination of a forward leg and vertical body produces a round lacking in subtlety (since the rider is using his seat to do what his legs should be doing and uses excess upper body movement to catch up with his horse on takeoff), at least this position allows a controlled performance. The jackknifed rider, on the other hand, is so poorly balanced that he is not able to use his arms, back, seat, or legs effectively enough to alter his horse's stride; and the weakness of his position puts him at the horse's mercy.

Third, while a rider who throws his upper body onto his horse's neck and lets his legs swing back is ahead of the horse's motion, one who jackknifes over a fence, letting his legs kick forward and his seat drop back into the saddle, is behind the motion. Since the rider ahead of the motion in the air is less likely to interfere with or physically abuse his horse, you shouldn't penalize him as heavily. Of course, you'll pin both of these riders lower than one who stays with the motion of his horse at all times.

A.

B.

Figs. 5-7A, B—On the approach to the obstacle (A), the rider's leg is kicked forward and his seat is in the saddle—instead of the leg properly remaining under him so he could rise into two-point position. At takeoff, he has pivoted on his knee, causing the lower leg to slide backward and his upper body to be ahead of the horse's motion in the air (B). Photographs by Pennington Galleries

For pinning purposes, the worst of the faults connected with a leg positioned too far forward is "getting left." Next is leaning the upper body forward over a leg that is kicked forward, both on the approach to the obstacle and in the air. Least severe of the three is approaching the fence with the leg forward and body on the vertical, then catching up with the horse in the air.

Legs Too Far Back

Not only do legs thrust forward cause problems, but so do legs drawn too far back along the horse's sides. A major form fault resulting from legs too far back is "perching," in which the upper body is ahead of the horses's motion at takeoff and in the air (Figs. 5-8A, B). Perching is penalized because: it throws excess weight onto the horse's front end as the animal is taking off from the ground and is airborne; it diminishes the rider's control, since he is ahead of the motion; and it affects the animal's balance, causing jumping faults such as front-end rubs and hanging (Figs. 5-9A, B).

A perching rider is particularly at risk aboard a horse that is prone to stopping at fences: when the rider gets ahead of his horse, a quick stop is likely to sling him forward into the jump. (This is why riders on green horses or stoppers should ride defensively by staying with—or, in extreme cases, behind—the motion on the approach to an obstacle.)

Although a rider usually perches because he is anxious to get over a fence, his putting his upper body ahead of the horse's motion in no way drives the animal over the obstacle. In fact, it has the opposite effect, since the rider's upper-body weight bearing down on the horse's forehand makes the animal question its ability to lift its front end off the ground and consider stopping or cheating (adding a stride at the base of the fence). However, perching is preferable to the faults connected with legs positioned too far forward (getting left, jackknifing the body, and suddenly shifting from behind to in front of the motion at takeoff), because the rider who perches is less radically out of balance than is one committing any of these other errors.

Form Faults Not Necessarily Related to Leg Position

Not only may riders whose legs are too far forward roach their backs to counterbalance themselves, but a rider with a good leg position may also roach his back, in which case the rounded back is usually an indication of assertive riding (Fig. 5-10A). The opposite fault is a swayback (or hollow back), which is seen mainly in beginners who are forcing their

A.

B.

Figs. 5-8A, B—At takeoff (A), and in the air (B), the rider's leg is too far back, causing his upper body to drop ahead of the horse's motion, a position known as "perching." Photographs by Pennington Galleries

A.

B.

Figs. 5-9A, B—When the weight of the rider's upper body is thrust onto the horse's front end, the animal may have resultant form faults, such as front end rubs (A) or hanging legs (B). Photographs by Pennington Galleries

A.

B.

Figs. 5-10A, B—The "roached back" (A), often indicative of an assertive rider, is not a serious fault as long as the rest of the rider's body is positioned correctly and used effectively. The "swayback" (B), usually associated with beginners, is also a minor error in the context of an overall good position. However, the stiffness of the swayback suggests a lack of relaxed communication between horse and rider that may lead to other errors during a round. Photographs by Pennington Galleries

bodies into position in an effort to maintain their balance in the air (Fig. 5-10B). As long as a rider's leg position is good, the swayback and roached back should only be penalized mildly, for although both detract from the elegance of the rider's appearance, neither affects the horse's balance significantly.

"Ducking," another upper-body fault, is characterized by the rider snapping his torso forward in the air so that his head is alongside the horse's neck at the zenith of the animal's arc (Fig. 5-11). Like perching, ducking is frequently a sign of an anxious rider—one who thinks he "needs to do something" with his upper body to get his horse over the fence. Also like perching, ducking has an effect just the opposite from the one intended; as the rider snaps forward in the air, he interferes with the horse's balance, making it more difficult for the animal to jump. For pinning purposes, ducking is worse than perching, since it is a more radical form of the rider being ahead of the horse's motion.

Fig. 5-11—This photograph clearly demonstrates why the habit of dropping the upper body beside the horse's neck is called "ducking." Besides thrusting excess weight onto the horse's front end, ducking also impairs the rider's vision. Photograph by Pennington Galleries

Looking back over the form faults discussed so far in this chapter, you would rank them, from most to least severe, as follows: (1) getting left over the fence—which is especially bad if the rider also catches the horse in the mouth; (2) jackknifing the body by kicking the legs forward and roaching the back on the approach to and in the air over an obstacle; (3) being behind the motion of the horse on the approach to the fence, then pivoting on the knee to catch up in the air; (4) ducking; (5) perching; and (6) roaching or hollowing the back—as long as a good leg position accompanied these upper-body faults.

Hands

While airborne, the rider has three appropriate options for hand position: (1) primary release—the basic release, in which the rider grabs his horse's mane as the animal jumps, giving himself both support for his upper body and assurance that he won't catch his horse in the mouth or get left in the air, no matter what happens; (2) secondary (or crest) release—the intermediate-level release, in which the rider rests his hands approximately a third of the way up the horse's neck, just below the mane, and presses down to provide support for his upper body and freedom for the horse's head and neck (Fig. 5-12A); and (3) jumping "out of hand"— the advanced method of release, in which the rider maintains contact with the horse's mouth as the horse leaves the ground, is airborne, and lands, so he can control the animal in the air (Fig. 5-12B).

Grabbing the mane is fine for beginners, but a rider past this stage should master the crest release, which will enable him to support his upper body by pressing into the horse's neck, rather than by hanging onto the mane. Once he masters the crest release, he may attempt jumping out of hand. This advanced release is necessary for riding difficult equitation courses that require the rider to be in control of his horse at each moment, even while airborne.

At the top of the horse's arc in the air, the rider's hand should be in either a direct line from the rider's elbow to the horse's mouth (Fig. 5-12B), or above this line, but should never be below it (Figs. 5-13A, B).

If the rider makes the mistake of underreleasing (also called "fixing the hand in the air"), he threatens the horse's balance, and the animal quickly learns that for its own safety, it should stop at the fence rather than attempt to jump it (Figs. 5-14A, B). In judging, impose a severe penalty on the rider who underreleases, causing his horse to struggle for balance, for in the realm of rider errors over fences, only getting left de-

A.

B.

Figs. 5-12A, B—The secondary release is marked by slack in the reins, allowing total freedom of the horse's head and neck (A). For the more advanced rider, jumping "out of hand" permits control of the horse in the air through rein contact (B). Photographs by Pennington Galleries

A.

B.

Figs. 5-13A, B—The hands may be above a direct line from the rider's elbow to the horse's mouth (A), but they must never be below this line (B). Photographs by Pennington Galleries

A.

B.

Figs. 5-14A, B—*Since horses naturally use their necks for balance in the air, a fixed hand that restricts this instinct will frustrate and intimidate an animal, causing it to "lose heart." While fixing the hand may be an obvious error (A), it can also be so subtle that you only notice the fault in the horse's slightly opened mouth and tense neck (B). Photographs by Pennington Galleries*

Fig. 5-15—*To have control of an animal throughout a course of fences, the rider must maintain a workable rein length, as pictured here. If the reins are too short, the upper body will be drawn forward into an ineffective position, ahead of the horse's motion. If the reins are too long, the rider's hands will end up against his stomach when he attempts to half-halt the horse, rendering his aids useless (see also Figures 4-21A and B). Photograph by A. O. White, Jr.*

serves a heavier penalty—since getting left is the only fault that makes it harder for the horse to keep its balance in the air.

Between fences, the rider's reins should be short enough for him to steer his horse easily—not so short that they cause the horse to overflex or the rider's body to be pulled forward, but not so long that the rider carries his hands in his lap (Fig. 5-15).

Eyes

The rider's eyes are his means of plotting his path from fence to fence and judging distances to the fences. When he uses his eyes properly, the rider looks ahead of where he is in the ring to line up his next set of fences, so he can travel on a logical path between obstacles.

Riders should envision a course as a series of lines (Fig. 5-16). For instance, in Figure 5-16, fences 1 and 2 form the first line, fences 3 and 4 form the second line, fences 5 and 6 form the third line, and fences 7 and 8 form the final line.

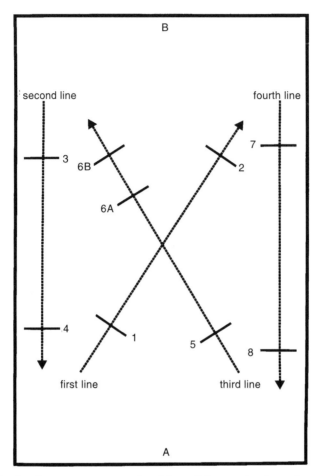

Fig. 5-16—*A course seen as a series of lines. Diagram by the author*

In properly using his eyes while riding this typical hunter course, the competitor looks toward fences 1 and 2 by point A, toward fences 3 and 4 by point B, toward fences 5 and 6 as he again reaches point A, and finally toward fences 7 and 8 as he gets to point B. Although the rider cannot visually line up the fences while he is still on the corners, the fact that his eyes are actively searching for a line enables him to find that line at the earliest place possible and gives him enough time to find a good distance to the fence.

The rider's ability to "find a good distance to a fence"—that is, to see as he approaches an obstacle how much he must adjust the horse's stride so the animal's feet will be placed at the correct distance from the fence for takeoff—is a combination of innate talent and practice. Some riders have a gift for finding a good distance several strides away from the fence and are naturally inclined to make the necessary adjustment of the horse's stride; while others think distances are elusive—easy to see on some occasions and very difficult at other times. (For this less talented rider, lots of practice adjusting the horses's stride between poles set on the ground, as well as practice over actual courses, will help him develop a better "eye" for a fence.) Whether the rider has natural talent or not, he must look to the upcoming fence soon enough to have time to adjust his horse's stride; for even those riders who judge distances with ease will make mistakes if they allow their horses' behavior or other circumstances to distract their eyes from the obstacles.

Having examined use of the eyes in connection with riding a very basic course, let us look at a more difficult course—one composed of several lines that have been used in Medal and Maclay finals in past years (Fig. 5-17). Walking this course beforehand, the rider should realize that if he tries to travel between fences 1 and 2 on a straight line (as shown by the dotted line in the diagram), he'll have to angle his horse so acutely across both fences that he'll risk a refusal or a runout. The better option is to ride straight over fence 1, keep the horse on a bending line around the turn, and jump fence 2 straight also.

From fence 2 to 3, the rider again can jump either on a bending line or on a straight line that angles his horse across both fences. Here the straight-line option presents two problems: (1) the angle at which both fences would have to be jumped is acute, and (2) the horse might think it is being steered into the railing on the far side of fence 3. The better option again would be the bending line: the horse jumps fence 2 straight across and takes a bending line between the fences that lets it jump fence 3 straight also. The bending line also gives the rider an advantage in placing the horse at the fence for takeoff: if the horse is not covering enough ground between fences, the rider can shave the corner and get to the third fence at the right point in the horse's stride; and if the animal is going to get to the fence too soon, the rider can use an inside leg to push the horse to the outside of the bend and make extra room for its stride.

Since the turns come quickly in this course, the rider should look for fence 2 while airborne over fence 1 and for fence 3 while in midair over fence 2. While the rider focuses on each upcoming fence, peripheral vision will keep him from wandering off his intended path between fences.

A few strides before point B, the rider begins looking for fence 4.

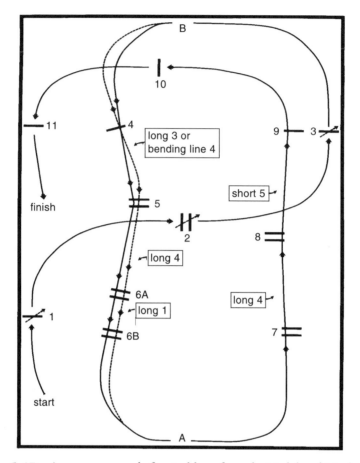

Fig. 5-17—A course composed of typical lines from the Medal and Maclay finals. Diagram by the author

Since this fence is not on the track but inside the ring, the rider should look toward the fence earlier than usual, for he needs time to plot his turn, line up the fences, and find a good distance to fence 4.

As mentioned in the chapter on Hunter Classes, the number of strides a horse should take between two fences often depends not only on those particular fences, but also on the fences that precede or follow them. The educated rider will realize that the most impressive route he can take for fences 4, 5, and 6A and 6B is to go straight between 4 and 5, turn in the air over fence 5 so the horse lands facing fences 6A and 6B, and move forward on a long stride into 6A, making it possible for the animal to go through the maximum-length in-and-out (6A and 6B) in one stride. He should shave the corner on the approach to 4 so his horse will be lined up to jump from the middle of 4 to the right-hand side of 5. In the air over fence 5, he looks toward fences 6A and 6B, with his hands and legs holding the horse straight between 5 and 6A so it won't lose precious footage by wandering to one side. (Note that centrifugal force will cause the horse to drift toward the left side of this line. The rider's hands and legs should compensate for this tendency.)

If the rider were on a short-strided horse and afraid his animal could not make the turn over fence 5 and have enough stride to get to fence 6A on time (since a turn in the air causes loss of momentum, which can be a serious problem on a short-strided horse), then he might consider adding a stride between fences 5 and 6A. However, this addition of a stride would cause lack of momentum that would spell trouble for the horse in the maximum-length in-and-out.

Suppose the rider tried to solve this problem another way—by adding a stride between fences 4 and 5, so he could ride on a bending line between them and approach fence 5 straight (see dotted line in Fig. 5-17). This would allow his horse to land facing fence 6A, so the animal would have taken off and landed straight, not losing any momentum in the air and, consequently, making the approach to fence 6A on a long stride possible. This option presents a satisfactory solution; but when comparing the difficulty of the options, you should realize that it is much harder for a rider to turn in the air over fence 5 than to take the bending-line option, which avoids the difficulty of reversing the direction of travel while airborne. The most difficult option is called the "winning option," for if everything else about the trips is equal, this difference in difficulty breaks the tie. For this reason, a competitor should not show a horse that has an extremely short stride if he wants to win in high-level competitions, for the horse's lack of an athletic stride will prohibit the rider from choosing the winning option.

After fences 6A and 6B, the rider looks for his next line by point A. Between fences 7 and 9 he must find as straight a line as possible, for the way these fences are set encourages a horse to drift. Since this line also involves going from a long distance to a short one, riding it well requires changing the horse's frame from an extended to collected one.

As the rider reaches point A, he should look to line up fences 7, 8, and 9, turning his horse for the approach to fence 7 as soon as he sees the right side of 8. Since the distance between 7 and 8 is long, the rider should move his horse forward in long strides from point A, so he will give himself the best opportunity to find a long spot to 7—which will enable the horse to leave long, land long, and cover the ground between 7 and 8 more easily.

For fences 7, 8, and 9, the line that allows the most fluid yet precise performance goes from the left side of fence 7 to the right side of 8 and back to the left side of 9. The distance between 8 and 9 is short, so between these fences the rider should bring his body back closer to the vertical, where his back can support his hands as he asks his horse to collect for the shorter strides necessary here. (If he realizes the horse is going to get to fence 9 too deep anyway, he can give the animal a little more room by using his left leg to press the horse toward the right side of the fence.)

As the rider lands over fence 9, he should keep his hands up, rather than collapsing onto them, so he can quickly collect his horse for the immediate approach to fence 10. Fence 10 is difficult because the turn to it is acute and the fence is set off the railing—a position that courts a runout. Active eyes that look for fence 10 while in midair over fence 9 and for fence 11 while airborne over fence 10, and an active hand and leg that collect and steer the horse are the keys to successful turns between these last three fences. (These turns are an example of places in a course at which the rider might need to resort to three-point contact in order to be precise.)

Throughout a course, the rider's eyes are inseparably linked with the execution of his plan. If he uses his eyes poorly—if, for instance, he looks too late toward upcoming lines—he'll overshoot turns and/or miss distances. These are major errors that indicate he is not "riding out a plan" and that he doesn't appreciate the importance of putting his horse at a safe takeoff point at every fence. You should penalize such mistakes heavily.

Landing

As a rider lands over a fence, his leg should maintain the same fixed position it held during the approach to the obstacle and in the air. His seat should remain out of the saddle, so it won't interfere with the animal's balance, and his upper body should stay with the horse's motion to the ground, rather than being ahead of or behind it (Fig. 5-18).

The worst leg fault a rider can commit on landing is letting the leg slip forward. This causes his seat to be thrust backward, behind the horse's motion, as the animal lands—a fault called "dropping back" (Fig. 5-19). As he drops back, the rider may yank his horse in the mouth and/

Fig. 5-18—This young rider is correctly keeping her heel down, leg on, and seat out of the saddle during landing. Photograph by Pennington Galleries

Fig. 5-19—On landing, this rider's leg has slipped forward, causing her seat to drop back into the saddle. Whether or not the rider's leg shifts in the air, if the seat touches the saddle before the horse has landed, the rider must be penalized for "dropping back." Photograph by Pennington Galleries

Fig. 5-20—When a rider's leg slips back, his upper body falls forward, and the excess weight on the horse's front end may cause jumping faults (such as the "cutting down" shown here). Photograph by Pennington Galleries

or hit it in the back with his seat; and for these abuses, as well as for the unsafe position the rider puts himself in by being radically behind the horse's motion, you should penalize this fault severely. (A rider whose leg slips forward only on landing isn't considered to have gotten left, since "getting left" refers to the rider being behind the horse's motion at take-off and/or at the peak of the jumping arc. The results of dropping back are similar to those of getting left; but dropping back is not penalized as severely because it presents a lesser chance of an accident, since the horse is almost on the ground when the fault occurs.)

Just as getting left and the leg slipping forward on landing are related, perching and the leg slipping backward on landing are related. Perching on takeoff and in midair places undue weight on the horse's front end, and the rider who perches at these points will generally maintain this overly forward position on landing. You will see him fall forward onto his hands for support, unable to support his upper body with his leg during landing (Fig. 5-20). As perching is preferable to getting left, the leg that slips backward on landing is preferable to the leg that slips forward, for the rider is at least with his horse as the animal lands, neither catching the horse in the mouth nor falling onto its back.

PERFORMANCE

General Observations

In an equitation class over fences, a rider should enter the ring with an aura of purpose, having prepared his horse by warming up over a few fences in the schooling area, and prepared himself by formulating his strategy for negotiating the obstacles. He should pick up a posting trot and maintain it until the horse completes the first quarter of the circle, at which time the rider sits the trot for a step or two and picks up the canter (Fig. 5-21). Immediately, he should assume two-point position and increase his horse's rhythm until the animal reaches a pace that is suitable for the size of the fences and the distances between them.

It is important for a rider to make his circle big enough, for a small figure will limit the horse's length of stride, as well as pace, and encourage the animal to lean inward to catch its balance. Necessary pace adjustments—such as squeezing the horse forward if it is too dull, or half-halting if it is trying to lengthen stride and increase its pace—should be made during the circle, with the pace for the entire course being established before the horse completes the circle, so the rider can concentrate on maintaining the proper pace, rather than on establishing it, throughout the course.

If the course is set in such a way that the rider cannot make the standard circle at the end of the ring, he must find another path that will allow him to accomplish the circle's aim—to establish pace. If he fails to do so, penalize him.

According to the *AHSA Rule Book*, the competitor may also circle at the completion of the round—which not only makes the trip more flowing, but also trains the horse to obediently pass the out-gate, rather than encouraging it to stop there. The final circle should be made at the same pace at which the round was ridden; and the downward transition that takes place before the horse leaves the ring should be forward and smooth, with the horse's hocks coming under it as the animal goes from the canter to the walk.

In an equitation class over fences, you seek many of the same qualities

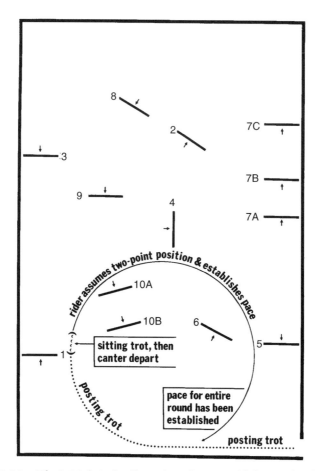

Fig. 5-21—The initial circle allows the rider to establish pace for the entire round. One of the major mistakes made by beginners is making the circle too small, so the horse never reaches the proper pace before the first fence. Diagram by the author

as in a performance on the flat: impulsion, bending, the horse being on the bit, collection in keeping with the difficulty of the test, and a look of discipline in both horse and rider. You should see no kicking, yanking, or clashing of aids (that is, aids working against one another); instead, the rider's legs, hands, and weight should be coordinated so well that they become "invisible aids" with the horse seeming to move around the course of its own volition. (Each competitor spends only a few seconds airborne during a class over fences, while the large remaining portion of the round is on the flat—that is, between fences. Consequently, flat work often makes the winning difference in competitions over fences as well as those entirely on the flat.)

Penalize riders whose coordination of aids is poor according to the area in which they are weak; assess the greatest penalties for weaknesses related to leg position and assign less heavy penalties to other faults, following the order of severity described in the previous chapter on position. Consider the rider's position and use of aids as they affect the horse's performance between fences and in the air; but don't penalize a rider for his horse's poor form unless the rider's position or actions seem to be the cause.

For instance, if a horse doesn't fold its legs tightly over a fence, but the rider has made no error that would seem to have caused this fault, you should not mark the rider lower for his horse's loose jumping form. If, however, the rider perches on his horse and puts it at a deep takeoff spot, his excessively forward position and poor placement of the horse could reasonably be considered responsible for the horse's poor jumping form, and the rider would be penalized.

Since it is the rider's responsibility to place the horse at a good takeoff spot, you should severely penalize riders who place their horses poorly, for a bad spot creates risks for both horse and rider. A rider who "misses the distance" and drives his horse into a poor spot deserves the greatest penalty, for he has not only chosen poorly, but has also forced his horse into this difficult position for takeoff. If a rider realizes the spot is not going to be good and unsuccessfully tries to adjust, the penalty you assess him for the bad spot shouldn't be as great as your penalty for the rider who seemed unaware his spot was bad and kept driving his horse into it. If a third competitor sees the spot is not going to be good and is successful in correcting it, but a little rough in doing so, penalize him less than either of the previous two. Finally, if a fourth rider sees he will not be able to get to the correct spot without an adjustment and manages to make it subtly, give him the best marks of the four.

Besides being responsible for the correct takeoff spot, the rider should be in control of the horse's leads during a course. If a horse is approaching a corner on the counter canter, the rider should ask the animal to do a flying change, so the horse will be balanced around the turn. (If the rider has difficulty performing the flying change, it would be smart for him to practice landing out of the air onto the correct lead, thereby avoiding the entire issue of flying changes in most instances. By applying an outside leg in the air, the rider can generally cause his horse to land on the inside lead; after a few practice sessions, most horses will land on the correct lead every time they're asked, as long as the rider is diligent about giving the aid and does so whenever the horse must land on a certain lead—that is, whenever the animal is negotiating a turn within the course or approaching a corner of the ring.)

Both the horse that performs the flying change prior to the corner and the horse that lands on the proper lead after a fence are correct; but horses that cross-canter or counter-canter the corners are incorrect. Penalize a cross canter around an entire corner more than a counter canter around an entire corner, for although the counter canter causes the horse to be unbalanced on the corner—and encourages the horse to drift to the outside of the turn on the approach to the fence—it is a normal sequence of the horse's feet and, therefore, does not look disjointed; whereas a cross canter around the entire corner causes the horse to be unbalanced, threatens the rider's safety when the horse attempts to jump from this disjointed gait, and looks terrible.

You should, however, pin a rider whose horse cross-canters only a few steps before switching to the correct lead above a rider whose horse counter-canters the entire corner. The issue is balance: the horse that cross-canters briefly before switching is on the correct lead for most of the corner and is balanced for takeoff, but the horse that counter-canters through the corner is unbalanced all the way around the turn and tends to drift to the outside on the approach to the upcoming fence.

Tests Over Fences

Test 6—"Pull up and halt (4 to 6 seconds)." Test 6 was formerly worded: "Pull up and halt between fences, except in combinations." This was recently changed to allow judges to call for the halt at other points in the course, for example, following the final line of fences. Although the new rule no longer spells out the restriction of this test in combinations, this is not to be construed as encouragement to call for the halt within a combination, for this practice in earlier years proved to be dangerous.

When Test 6 is applied within a line of fences, it separates riders who simply pose on their horses from those who can use their positions to achieve full control of their animals. The difficulty of the test lies in the horse seeing the upcoming fence and being anxious to jump it—particularly if an animal that gets "on the muscle" is asked to do this test toward the end of the course, or if the horse is asked to halt facing the in-gate and wants to get back to the herd.

Ideally, Test 6 should be performed promptly yet smoothly, with the horse keeping its hocks well under its body during the downward transition. While halting, the horse should stand squarely and be on the bit, prepared for any further testing. If the halt is to be followed by the horse jumping the upcoming fence from the walk, trot, or canter, the rider should stop the horse far enough away from the obstacle for the animal to have time to realize it is being asked to jump when a gait is resumed following the halt.

In testing inexperienced riders, look for smoothness and promptness in the downward transition and stillness in the horse at the halt. In judging higher-level riders, you should see the horse collected into a medium frame and on the bit, as well.

Test 7—"Jump obstacles on figure eight course." Use this test to measure the rider's ability to get the horse to *land on the correct lead after a fence*, to *perform flying changes*, or to *jump fences on an angle* (Figs. 5-22A, B).

As the first course is set (Fig. 5-22A), the best option is to land on the proper lead out of the air, rather than attempt flying changes on the turns. To go from fence 1 to fence 2, the rider should apply left leg pressure in the air over fence 1, asking the horse to land on the right lead so that it will be balanced on the approach to fence 2. In the air over fence 2, he should use right leg pressure to ask the horse to land on the left lead, to assure a balanced approach to fence 3.

Although landing on the left lead is the better option after fence 3, a horse that lands on the right lead can perform a flying change at point A and still have a smooth performance, since there is enough space between fences 3 and 4 for either option. (The rider should make a flying change just as his horse starts into a corner. If the change occurs after the horse is in the turn, mark it as having been made late.)

Negotiating fences 4, 5, and 6, the rider should ask the horse to land on the left lead over fence 4 and on the right lead over 5. He again has the option of landing on the right lead over 6 or performing a flying change (by point B) if his horse doesn't land on the proper lead.

A rider who cannot get his horse to land on a particular lead is at a great disadvantage in this test, since a horse that lands on the wrong lead must either counter-canter to the next fence—and have its balance threatened—or collect and perform a flying change, which costs precious footage in competition where the distances are set long. In addition, when a rider has to concern himself with a flying change, his concentration on the distance to the upcoming fence is interrupted.

When the fences are set next to the railing (Fig. 5-22A), the flying

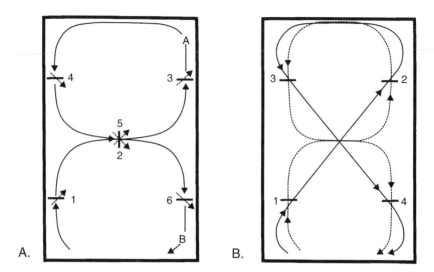

Fig. 5-22A, B—In Course A, the solid line traces the logical path for negotiating these obstacles, while the dotted line shows the option of jumping fences at an angle—a poor option in this case, because the fences are set so close to the railing. In Course B, the solid line marks the path for jumping obstacles on an angle, while the dotted line shows the route that would be taken if the rider decided to demonstrate flying changes across the center line. Diagrams by the author

change is the only option for a rider who can't get his horse to land on a desired lead dependably; but when the fences are set away from the railing (Fig. 5-22B), the rider may choose either to perform a flying change on the center line or to jump the fences at an angle, with no change of leads across the middle of the ring. Both options have their drawbacks, for although flying changes disrupt length of stride for a few seconds and make finding a good distance to the next fence more difficult, jumping fences at an angle increases the likelihood of runouts and knockdowns. Since angling the fences is the riskier choice, you should give credit to the rider who carries out this more difficult option successfully.

Test 8—"Ride without stirrups or drop and pick up stirrups." Not only should a rider appear as secure without stirrups as with them, he should also be able to "get the job done" as well. Without stirrups in a class over fences, the rider's body should be positioned generally the same as it was when he had his feet in the irons. The only significant difference is that without support from his stirrups, it is acceptable for the rider to maintain a "modified three-point" position between the fences, rather than two-point—that is, his crotch will be touching the saddle, and his body will be inclined 10 degrees in front of the vertical, rather than 20 degrees. At the fence, however, he must hold his seat out of the saddle during takeoff, while in the air, and on landing, so he won't interfere with the horse's back. (The rider may also use "extreme three-point" position at particularly difficult places in the course, such as during tight turns or short distances; but he should not maintain this extreme position—with his upper body on the vertical and seat riveted in the saddle—during the entire course.)

Test 8 is not frightening to an experienced, fit athlete who believes he can turn in a trip without stirrups that is comparable to one with them; but it can be an alarming test for a weak, inexperienced rider who is afraid he will not be able to stay on without stirrups. For this reason, Test 8 should be reserved for advanced riders. (See also Equitation on the Flat: Tests.)

Test 9—"Jump low obstacles at a walk and trot as well as at a canter. The maximum height for a walk obstacle is 3 feet. The maximum height and spread for a trotting obstacle is 3 feet." By asking a rider to walk or trot a fence within a course, you can further test his control of the horse and his timing to the fences. No matter what gait the horse is in, the rider should look for a distance to the obstacle and adjust the horse's steps to help the animal meet the proper takeoff point. The trot provides a better test of the rider's timing than the walk, for at the trot the rider must have quicker coordination in monitoring each of the horse's steps on the approach to the fence.

Faults that can be committed by riders during Test 8 are, from most to least severe: (1) allowing the horse to refuse the fence; (2) "getting left" in the air; (3) letting the horse break gait on the approach to the fence— for instance, the common error of allowing the horse to canter the last step or two at a "trot fence"; and (3) "jumping up on the horse's neck"— that is, getting ahead of the horse's motion at takeoff.

Test 15—"Change horses. This test is the equivalent of two tests." Although Test 15 is popular in high level competitions, such as the Medal and Maclay finals, it should be used with discretion, for a young rider on a strange horse is a combination which lends itself to uncertain results. The fact that the rider was forced to get on an unfamiliar horse in order to complete the competition is legally questionable in the event the child is injured; and, in addition, there is the problem of fairness in putting riders on horses that may not be trained as well as their own.

Since it is common knowledge that horses must be trained in order to give proper responses to the rider's aids, it should also be recognized that the rider who has put in the most time and effort on his mount and has refined his animal's responses to the aids will be at a disadvantage when he has to compete on another rider's horse that is not trained as well and, therefore, is not as responsive to the rider. Although the better rider would be able to improve his competitor's horse if given time to work the animal, it can hardly be expected of the rider to remake the horse while competing over the course and to produce the beautiful round he is capable of making on his own mount. In effect, then, the lesser rider is given the advantage during a switch, for he is handed the better-trained horse and can "cash in" on his competitor's talent and effort.

Much is left up to fate in Test 15, for many of the rider's considerations in planning his performance on his own horse are wasted when he has to get on another person's horse. For instance, the smart rider will have chosen a horse that suits his build and dressed himself to look attractive on that horse; but when he is asked to switch onto another animal, his build may not suit the horse's conformation and his clothing may look ugly with the horse's coloring. If his competitor has been lucky enough not to have these problems, then the mismatched horse-rider combination is at a disadvantage even before the ride-off has begun.

Since Test 15 is being used today, however, we must consider what it is intended to prove. The idea behind this test is that a good rider can switch onto various horses and ride them all well, while a mediocre rider may be able to ride his own horse well but will not be capable of getting on a strange horse and turning in a trip of equal quality.

When you call for this test, judge the rider's position and performance by the criteria you use when considering riders on their own horses. Riders who get into a problem with a strange horse but attempt to correct it should place above those who have trouble but passively allow the horse to be in control. This theory holds true whether the rider is on his own horse or on an unfamiliar animal: the rider who recognizes a problem and attempts to correct it should be rewarded for his knowledge and effort by being pinned above the rider who does nothing when placed in a similar situation. Of course, better than these two would be the rider who turns in such a good trip on a strange horse that he looks as though he's ridden the animal all his life. This would be the ideal rider in Test 15.

6

WHAT TO EXPECT FROM EQUITATION RIDERS

BEGINNERS

As mentioned numerous times throughout this book, the most important feature of a rider's position is his leg. In judging a class of beginners on the flat or over fences, reward riders who have worked hard to develop good leg position and who use their legs properly to propel the horse forward—squeezing, rather than kicking the animal. All abuses (for example, yanking the horse in the mouth, kicking it in the sides, or getting left over the fence) are severely penalized, for it is at this elementary level that riders must learn to be sensitive to horses as living beings, and nothing brings this home as well as losing a class. Intentional abuse, such as jerking or kicking out of anger, should be penalized more than inadvertent abuse, for example, getting left in the air and grabbing mane in an effort to stay off the horse's mouth.

As for use of the crop, it is better if a rider can keep his horse going forward without the use of a stick; but it is preferable for a beginner to use his stick to keep the horse moving than to hesitate to use it and let the horse break gait (on the flat or over fences), add a stride between fences, or stop at an obstacle. As long as the rider uses the stick properly—that is, on the horse's flesh just behind the rider's leg; in degree appropriate to the severity of the disobedience; and timed properly with the occurrence of the fault—the use of the stick is not a major fault in a class of beginners. If a rider uses the stick anywhere in front of the saddle, however, he should be severely penalized for improper use of this artificial aid.

Generally speaking, beginners should not wear spurs, for most of them don't have the stationary leg position to be able to wear spurs without accidentally abusing the horse. However, if a beginner wears spurs and uses them properly—that is, uses them only when needed and doesn't stab the horse in the sides, but rather presses the spurs into the flesh—he should not be penalized.

If the rider uses voice commands—such as "whoa"—to slow the horse down, his voice should be so soft that it is audible only to the horse, not to the judge. Loud commands should be penalized at even this beginning level, for equitation is founded on the concept of nonverbal communication between rider and horse. Most annoying is the competitor who provides a running commentary during his performance. His accounts are intended to convince onlookers that it is not he and his poor job of riding, but rather the horse that is responsible for the terrible performance. Comments such as, "Come on, Salty. We've done this lots of times before," uttered as the horse stops at the fence, indicate that the rider is not concentrating on his performance, but is unduly concerned with what spectators think of him as he finds himself in this embarrassing situation. Penalize the orator severely.

Clucking to encourage a horse forward should be used discreetly, for a rider who clucks around the entire course demonstrates the ineffectiveness of his leg. A cluck from a rider at a single difficult place in the course should not be penalized; but if clucking is noticeably a habit, it should be faulted. In comparing the cluck to talking, however, talking is ten times worse, for it is completely out of the realm of what the rider should be doing.

In all levels of equitation competition, riders must be able to get the proper diagonals and leads. If a beginner picks up the wrong diagonal or lead but corrects the mistake immediately, he should be penalized only mildly, for it is obvious he knows what he should be doing. If, however, a beginner goes around the ring for long periods of time and does not realize he is on the wrong diagonal or lead, he must be severely penalized.

When performing the canter depart, the beginner must not lean over his horse's shoulder to throw the horse on the lead or to check for the correct lead. In checking both leads and diagonals, he should keep his upper body in the center of the horse and tilt only his head (or, preferably, keep his head up and let his eyes glance down) to check the motion of the horse's leg—the outside foreleg for diagonals, the inside foreleg for leads. Give a heavier penalty to the rider who leans over his horse's shoulder to throw it on the lead, than to one who leans to check the diagonal or lead.

In judging beginners, you are looking for riders who have a clear understanding of "reward" and "punishment." In simplest terms, punishment is the use of any of the natural or artificial aids, and reward is the lack of punishment. When the rider squeezes the horse forward with his leg (natural aid), or encourages the horse forward with his stick (artificial aid), he is punishing the horse for not going forward at the desired pace. As soon as the horse achieves the proper pace, the rider relaxes his aids as a means of reward. Similarly, if the rider squeezes his hand muscles (natural aid) in an attempt to slow the horse down, then the hand is a punishment. As the horse slows down, the hand muscles relax as a reward to the animal. It is important for a beginner to practice the separation of driving aids—such as the leg and stick—from restraining aids—such as pressure on the reins—so he won't "clash aids" by simultaneously asking the horse for opposing responses.

In higher levels of riding, the concept of reward and punishment becomes more difficult for the rider to comprehend when he is told to collect his horse by using what would appear to be two opposing aids— leg pressure, to create impulsion in the haunches, and hand pressure, to half-halt the horse in order to balance its front end. However, a talented rider, through much "trial and tribulation" on the flat, will eventually understand how the principles of reward and punishment hold true at even the highest level of riding; and, using this knowledge, he will be able to produce the maximum quality performance with minimum anxiety in the horse.

When judging the beginner, however, we are not expecting collection, but are mostly concerned with the rider's basic understanding of reward and punishment as it relates to simple tasks. A beginner should know not to use the gas pedal (leg) and brakes (hand) at the same time. He should realize that to turn a horse to the right, he must ease off of the left rein, and vice versa. Basically, he must understand how to avoid fighting himself, so he can prevent the clashing of aids from leading to a battle with his horse.

In all levels of riding, a good motto is: "Do only what it takes to get what you want." This is particularly pertinent to beginners, who are apt to kick or jerk before they have attempted to squeeze.

INTERMEDIATE RIDERS

By "intermediate riders," I don't mean competitors who show in classes restricted by twelve wins or less; rather, this term is used loosely to encompass all riders past the beginner stage, but not up to an advanced level. By the intermediate stage, a rider's position should be well founded, offering security and allowing him to be effective. Not only should he be able to perform at the walk, trot, canter, and hand gallop around the ring, but also he should be capable of riding basic school figures, such as a serpentine or figure eight with a simple change of leads.

At this stage, the rider should not have to resort to his stick to reinforce a weak leg, but should only go to the stick if the horse commits a serious error—such as refusing a fence or persistently adding a stride at the base of obstacles. If he has any doubt his horse will approach each obstacle willingly, he should wear spurs (as well as carry a stick) so he can use this more subtle aid before resorting to the obvious.

An intermediate rider should check the diagonal or lead by glancing, rather than tilting his head, if he is not able to feel whether he is right or wrong. If the rider picks up the wrong lead or diagonal, he should be severely penalized for making these elementary mistakes—although he can redeem himself somewhat if he immediately notices the error and corrects it. (Since it is easier for a rider to feel he has the wrong lead or diagonal on a corner—because the turn makes the lack of balance more obvious—you should penalize a competitor who travels on the wrong lead or diagonal on the straightaway and does not notice his mistake until he is in the corner more than one who is able to recognize the problem while still on the straightaway.)

At the intermediate level, a rider should be able to keep his horse on the rail by holding it there with his inside leg, rather than leading it there with an outside opening rein. He should be able to bend his horse, keep a steady rhythm at the various gaits, make smooth upward and downward transitions, and maintain contact on the animal's mouth and sides on the flat and between fences.

During a course, he should try to place his horse at a safe takeoff spot, rather than let the horse get there "any old way," as beginners—who are mainly preoccupied with staying on—are likely to do. On course, he should look as though he is trying to ride out a plan. At this stage, the crest release, rather than grabbing mane, would be appropriate in the air.

ADVANCED RIDERS

You should expect a great deal more from advanced riders than from intermediate-level competitors. Not only should an advanced rider be able to maintain steady contact with the horse's mouth and sides, he should also collect his horse into a medium frame for the basic flat tests—walk, trot, and canter—and lengthen or shorten the frame for more difficult tests, such as those required in the USET Equitation Class or included in Tests 1–19.

Emphasis on performance increases at this level because many advanced riders have attractive, as well as secure, positions, so the deciding factor becomes quality of performance. On the flat, an advanced rider's horse should move forward with impulsion and stay on the bit at all times. From head to tail, it should be slightly bent in the direction of travel on the corners of the ring and straight in its body on the long sides of the arena. An incorrect diagonal or lead is inexcusable at this level, for the rider should feel the error coming and correct the problem before it is visible to the judge. Even one step of the wrong diagonal or lead, showing lack of feeling in the rider, is penalized. An advanced rider should concentrate on his horse's source of power—its haunches—and keep the hocks engaged by coordinating leg pressure and half-halts. If the rider is insensitive in doing this, his horse's angry expression will point out the problem to you.

When riding a course of fences, the advanced competitor should have a plan and adhere to it as much as possible, only making alterations where unforeseen problems necessitate them. You should take into consideration the riders' strategies when comparing two trips of similar quality and give credit to the one who chooses the more difficult options in a course. Riders at this level should be "jumping out of hand," so they can control their horses in the air as well as on the ground, making the difficult options feasible.

In addition to displaying all the desirable features discussed in the equitation chapters, the advanced rider's performance should demonstrate one more significant quality: empathy between horse and rider. When watching horse and rider, you should feel that they are working together for a common goal, that the animal is not just being obedient to a master, but that it is performing with "heart," trying to please the person whose words it cannot understand, but whom it understands just the same.

7

THE JUDGE'S CARD

NUMERICAL SCORING

There are three types of symbols used in marking the judge's card: abbreviations, hieroglyphics, and numbers. Limited time and space make these symbols necessary, for if you try to use longhand, you will not have as much time to watch the performance and your card will be messy and confusing.

Abbreviations are made up mostly of consonants suggesting the word or words that describe an error—such as "Tw" for *twist,* or "LF" for *loose form.* When using abbreviations, capitalize only the first letter of a word, so that it will be clear whether your consonants are part of one word, as in the case of "Twist," or of two words, as in "Loose Form" (see list of abbreviations beginning on page 209).

Hieroglyphics are pictorial representations of your comments. These lines, dots, arrows, and other symbols will not only save space but also make the card easier to read than if you try to use abbreviations alone.

At the completion of each round, when you have finished using abbreviations and hieroglyphics to record your observations, give the performance a numerical score (Figs. 7-1A, B). If the score is 75 or above, place it on a separate sheet of paper and write the rider's number next to the score, so that at the end of the class you will immediately be able to give the results to the announcer (Fig. 7-2). If you do not have enough scores above 75 to pin the class, refer to your card and list the next highest scores until you reach the number of placings you need (eight numbers for classes requiring a jog and six for classes not requiring a jog, unless the prize list states otherwise). At the other extreme, if you have an abundance of horses scoring above 75, you can adjust your cutoff point higher during the class.

Many shows provide a walkie-talkie or head-set, so the judge can call in the placings to the announcer. If, however, you have to send the results through a runner, write down your list again and send the copy, so that you will have a list in hand for the jog. Do not write the results at the top of your card until you have finished judging the jog, for a lame horse will change all the placings below it.

Basically, numerical scoring is patterned after the scoring system used at schools:

90s Excellent A
80s Good   B
70s Fair   C
60s Poor   D
50s Failing F

Think of a score of 90 as a "basic ceiling," with only a horse of exceptional ability—that is, one that is both an excellent jumper and an excellent mover—being able to score above this mark. You also want to think of 95 as an "absolute ceiling," so that your scores will not reach too close to the real ceiling of 100. By trying to cap the scores at 95, you still have a little room in case you are faced with scoring a number of outstanding trips in the 90s. (This is a problem only at the largest shows in the country.)

Reserve scores above 90 for horses of excellent quality that turn in wonderful trips. For horses that have inherent limitations, the scores should never move above 90. Some examples of this are horses that are good jumpers and good movers, but are not excellent in either category; horses that are excellent movers, but only adequate jumpers; and horses that are excellent jumpers, but only adequate movers. With the very best trip each of these could turn in, their scores would never go beyond 90. When ridden well, these are the horses that score in the 80s.

To score in the 70s, a good horse—that is, a good jumper and good mover—would have to make some substantial errors. Untalented horses, however, can easily fall into the 70s. A poor mover would not have to have many jumping faults to reach the 70s, and a horse with chronically

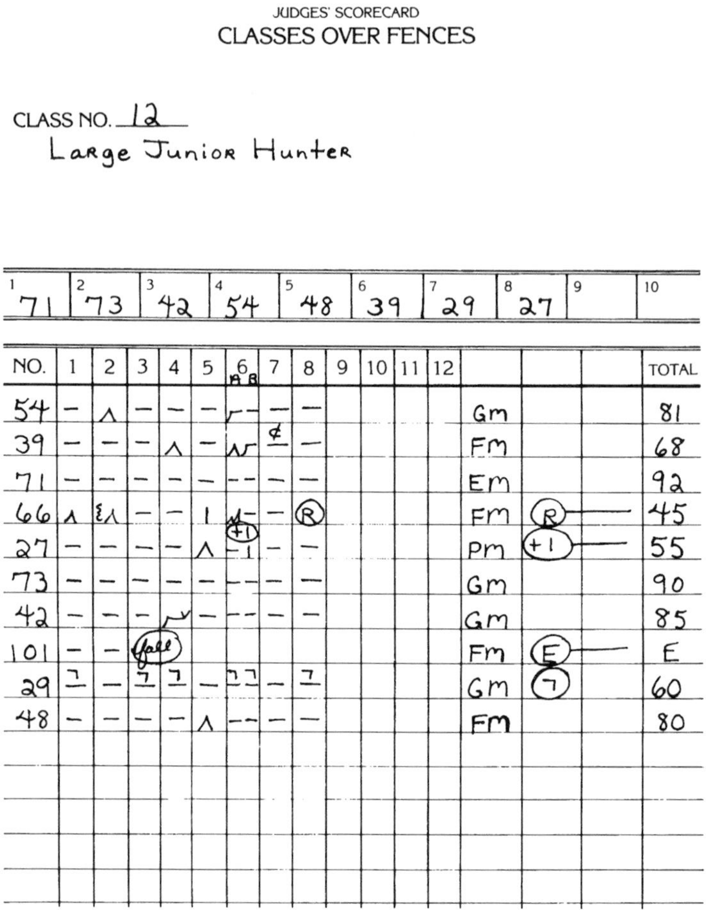

JUDGES' SCORECARD
CLASSES OVER FENCES

CLASS NO. _12_

Large Junior Hunter

1	2	3	4	5	6	7	8	9	10
71	73	42	54	48	39	29	27		

NO.	1	2	3	4	5	6	7	8	9	10	11	12				TOTAL
54	–	∧	–	–	–	–	–	–					Gm			81
39	–	–	–	∧	–	∧	¢	–					Fm			68
71	–	–	–	–	–	–	–	–					Em			92
66	∧	ƐΛ	–	–	1	–	–	Ⓡ					Fm	Ⓡ		45
27	–	–	–	–	∧	–1	–	–					Pm	(+1)		55
73	–	–	–	–	–	–	–	–					Gm			90
42	–	–	–	✓	–	–	–	–					Gm			85
101	–	–	(fall)										Fm	Ⓔ		E
29	⅂	–	⅂	⅂	–	⅂⅂	–	⅂					Gm	⑦		60
48	–	–	–	–	∧	–	–	–					Fm			80

Fig. 7-1A—The mock card above shows symbols and scores as they might appear in a Large Junior Hunter class. Compare these symbols and scores to those in Fig. 7-1B, which shows the same trips when scored as an Equitation Over Fences class.

poor form in the air would have no trouble falling to the 70s or below.

The 60s and 50s represent very bad trips. Most judges have a set of predetermined scores to use for common major errors. I have provided a chart comparing these predetermined scores for hunter and equitation classes, since the division rules differ. Asterisks (*) identify equitation scores that differ from hunter scores.

JUDGES' SCORECARD
CLASSES OVER FENCES

CLASS NO. __15__

Equitation Over Fences (15-17)

1	2	3	4	5	6	7	8	9	10
73	71	29	42	54	39				

NO.	1	2	3	4	5	6 BB	7	8	9	10	11	12				TOTAL
54	–	I↓ ∧	–	–	–	r–	–	–					GP			79
39	–	–	–	∧	–	∧	∅ –	–					FP			72
71	–	–	–	–	–	– –	–	–					GP			90
66	∧	³∧	–	–	1	∦– ④①	–	Ⓡ					FP	Ⓡ—		.45
27	–	–	–	–	∧	–1	–	–					FP	⊕1 —		55
73	–	–	–	–	–	– –	–	–					EP			92
42	–	–	–	↵	–	– –	–	–					FP			80
101	–	–	⟨fall⟩										PP	Ⓔ—		E
29	–	–	–	–	–	– –	–	–					FP			85
48	↗	↗	–	–	↗∧	– –	↗	–					PP	⟨↗⟩		67

Fig. 7-1B—Notice that the riders' general position between fences and specific position errors over fences affect the equitation scores in Fig. 7-1B, while the horses' general way of moving and specific form errors over fences affect the hunter scores in Fig. 7-1A.

Note: According to the *AHSA Rule Book*, in the Equitation Division, "The following constitute major faults and can be cause for elimination: (a) a refusal; (b) loss of stirrup; (c) trotting while on course when not part of a test; and (d) loss of reins." However, I have never known any of these to be penalized by elimination. Usually, they are scored as follows.

Hunter

Trotting on course   60
Very poor trip   51–59
Dangerous fence   55
Adding a stride
   in an in-and-out   55

Knockdown   50

1 Refusal   45
2 Refusals   35
3 Refusals   *Elimination*
Fall   *Elimination*
Off course   *Elimination*

Equitation

Trotting on course   60
Very poor trip   51–59
Dangerous fence   55
Adding a stride
   in an in-and-out   55
*Loss of stirrup   55
*Loss of reins   55
*Knockdown (penalize at judge's
   discretion)

1 Refusal   45
2 Refusals   35
3 Refusals   *Elimination*
Fall   *Elimination*
Off course   *Elimination*

For "trotting on course" to receive a 60, there must be a clear break from the canter, not just a skip behind. The late Gene Cunningham, a well-respected horseman and judge, used to say, "If you can't post to it, it isn't a trot." A skip behind—that is, a break of gait in the hind feet, but not in the front—is penalized at the judge's discretion.

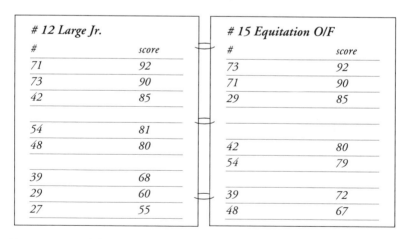

# 12 Large Jr.	
#	score
71	92
73	90
42	85
54	81
48	80
39	68
29	60
27	55

# 15 Equitation O/F	
#	score
73	92
71	90
29	85
42	80
54	79
39	72
48	67

Fig. 7-2—It is helpful to have a separate sheet of paper on which the top scores can be listed in proper pinning order. The sheet on the left shows the pinning list for the Large Junior Hunter class in Fig. 7-1A, while the sheet on the right shows the pinning list for the Equitation Over Fences class in Fig. 7-1B.

For a "very poor trip" to receive a score between 51 and 59, it should be so bad that if you deducted points for all the errors, the score would be 50 or less. You stop at 50 to make sure you don't score a bad trip below one that had a knockdown (exception: equitation classes) or refusal.

When an automatic score of 55 is assigned because of the way a single fence was jumped, the obstacle must have been jumped so dangerously that it made you gasp! This is not just a risky spot but one that nearly "bought the farm" for the rider's family.

Other than giving these predetermined scores for major errors, you arrive at a numerical score based on the deduction of points for each error committed. Do not deduct for the error as it occurs, but use the symbols previously discussed to "draw a picture" of the way the course is ridden, so that later you can bring each trip to mind if you need to—for instance, if two or more horses have the same score and you have to break the tie. At the end of each trip, starting with a score of 90, deduct points for errors committed. Use a 5-point deduction for a medium-deep spot as the standard around which all other scores are based.

For horses that are in the category of excellent jumpers and movers, scores above 90 will be based on "plus points." These are additional points added to reflect the quality of performance. Again, you are thinking of 95 as an "absolute ceiling," so do not get carried away and score too high when you get your first really good trip in a class.

Too many horses scoring in the 90s is not the usual problem for judges. Most will be dealing with a number of scores in the 80s and 70s, or possibly below. It will suffice to put a series of plusses if you find you have too many horses scoring the same. (For Classics, just hold up your score, even if it is the same as an earlier one, for the announced score is the average from the two or three judges present. Even at small shows that hold a Classic-type competition using only one judge, there is no problem in holding up the same score as for a previous trip because the final score will be the average of each horse's scores for the two rounds).

It is helpful in judging classes over fences to put a circle around a major error—such as a refusal, a knockdown, an added stride in an in-and-out, trotting on course, or elimination—and to make note of it in your space for comments following the trip, so that you will make "double sure" not to overlook the error in tallying your score. If the competition is terrible and/or the class very small, you may have to pin a horse that has a major fault, such as a knockdown or refusal, but generally these faults would put a hunter out of the ribbons. Of course, an eliminating fault—such as a third refusal or a fall—must not be pinned even if there are ribbons left over.

In numerical scoring, as with everything else, practice makes perfect. If you use this system all the time, you will not feel uncomfortable when your score is displayed to the public during a Classic.

Back-to-Back Classes

Back-to-back classes are two hunter classes in the same division and section that are held simultaneously in a ring. The rider can perform over the first course, stay in the ring, then perform over the second course; or he can leave after the first trip and come back later to ride the second course. This format is intimidating to novice judges, for it requires scoring intermittently on two cards.

Here are a few tips to make judging back-to-back classes easier:

1. Number your cards with a large "1" or "2" in the top left-hand corner so that you can easily locate each card for the first and second trip.

2. At the top of each card, draw a line representing the first fence, placing it at the correct angle in the ring and drawing an arrow to show the direction in which it should be jumped. Also, write what type of fence it is. This will help you know if the horse is starting over the wrong fence or if you are about to score the performance on the wrong card.

3. Write the courses out at the top of the cards. For instance, outside-inside-outside-inside would tell you the horse should jump the line of fences next to the rail, a diagonal line, a second line of fences next to the rail, and a final diagonal line. Even simpler is a course with an outside line, two diagonal lines, and a final outside line. It can be marked out-side-8-outside, with the "8" describing the shape formed by the two diagonal   lines.

4. If you are judging a class and think a horse is performing over the wrong course, but are not sure, keep scoring the animal wherever you started writing. You can check your cards at the end of the trip to see if the horse was off course or if you started scoring on the wrong card. If the error was yours, go ahead and write the horse's number on the proper card, assign a numerical score, and transfer the symbols later as you have time. Remember to strike the number and symbols from the wrong card so that you won't pin the horse in the wrong class.

5. Keep a small notebook on hand that you can use for judging back-

to-back classes, so that the first round is always on a page to the left and the second round on the page to the right. At the top of each page, mark "score" to the left and "#" to the right, so that you can place the numerical score first, then locate the rider's number and mark it beside the score.

General Impressions

In both hunter and equitation classes, there will be space on the judge's card for "comments" just after the numbered boxes designating each jump. For hunters, this space should be used to mark the horse's general way of going: "EM" for excellent mover, "GM" for good mover, "FM" for fair mover, and "PM" for poor mover. Coupled with the specific markings in the boxes, these comments give you the complete story of the horse's performance. For horses that are only "fair" or "poor" movers, deduct points in addition to the points deducted for jumping errors. A "poor mover" would receive about a 10-point deduction; a "fair mover" would receive about a 5-point deduction; a "good mover" would receive no deducted points; and an "excellent mover" would receive from about 1 to 3 "plus points" according to how well it moved.

In judging equitation classes, the area for "comments" is used to re-mark on the rider's basic position, which includes not only how he sits but how he uses his aids: "EP" for excellent position, "GP" for good position, "FP" for fair position, and "PP" for poor position. These general impressions enable you to consider not only the riders' position over the fences but also their basic riding ability on course. "Poor position" describes the rider who has few, if any, of the basics; "fair position" describes the rider who has a minimal number of position errors or whose angles are good, but who is weak or a little loose; "good position" describes the rider who is basically correct and effective in the use of his position; and "excellent position" describes the rider who is built beautifully, has the correct position, and is effective with his aids—a rider with "style." Riders with a "fair" or "poor" position should have points deducted in addition to those reflecting their position over fences. A "poor" rider receives about a 10-point deduction, a "fair" rider receives a 5-point deduction, a "good" rider receives no point deduction, and an "excellent" rider receives between 1 and 3 "plus points" according to the quality of his riding.

You can make comments to help yourself remember each horse or rider, but never write the riders' or horses' names. If an exhibitor asks to see a judge's card, a name beside a number might give the impression that the judge is relying on a competitor's reputation, as well as on the performance, to pin the class. Markings that designate physical appearance (such as "Tl Gl" for "tall girl," or "Bg Gry" for "big gray" horse) or that indicate chronic problems (such as "LL" for "loose legs") are beneficial in helping the judge recall particular riders.

Judges on Judging

Since hunter seat riding has become such an expensive and competitive sport, riders, trainers, and owners tend to be more vocal about poor judging than in years past. They come to the show with the expectation that the best performances will be pinned, and if they feel the judge is incompetent or dishonest, they are angry that their money and efforts are being wasted.

George Morris believes that the judge owes the competitor three things: knowledge of the subject, good bookkeeping, and total honesty. Michael Page elaborates: "The foremost consideration of a judge is using his knowledge and experience, based on a thorough understanding and application of the rules for the particular class. He must have a system of judging which reflects his impartial consideration on those factors in a clearly professional manner."

"Knowledge" is not simply knowing the rules set forth by the AHSA, but also understanding the various aspects of performance of horse and rider and how they should be scored.

"In my opinion," says Daniel Lenehan, "there is no way that a person can learn to judge solely by reading a book or attending a clinic or two. After forty years of judging, I still find myself confronted with situations that are without precedent. Nothing can ever take the place of actual experience gained by judging with knowledgeable people."

"Good bookkeeping"—the ability to maintain an accurate and easily readable judge's card—is extremely important, because if you can't keep track of your comments concerning each horse, you're in trouble, especially during a large class. For classes over fences, score each fence; but for flat classes, the less you write the better.

Referring to judging flat classes, Stephen Hawkins says, "Do it all in your head. If you have to write, you lose too much viewing time. Work the horses one way of the ring; reverse and write the order of preference during the trot (and sitting trot in an equitation class); and finish the order prior to the final canter. Then adjust the placings as the horses line up, according to mistakes made at the canter."

Finally, judges should have integrity and not be swayed by personal friendships or politics. They must put the interests of the sport above their own and have the character to make impartial decisions and stand by them.

You may find the following lists of abbreviations and hieroglyphics helpful in marking a judge's card. Since there is no official set of marks that judges are required to use, each judge makes up his or her own system for scoring. The lists are a compilation of marks submitted by several judges, and the "examples" that follow some of them are provided to show where certain marks are placed in relation to others—that is, above, to the side of, or below.

FAULTS OVER FENCES

good spot   —

long spot   ⌐⌐

cutting down   ∨

example: ⌐∨

reaching   ⌐→

diving   ⋀↘

dangerous
(i.e., "risky," as in flailing legs or other desperate and   Ⓓ
unorthodox jumping attempts)

quick off the ground   ℺

example: ℺⌐

deep spot   ⋀

very deep spot |

refusal   Ⓡ

example: Ⓡ Ⓡ —

elimination   Ⓔ————————

example: Ⓡ Ⓡ Ⓔ————

hanging one leg   ⌐

example: ⌐
            ∧

hanging two legs   ⊓|

example: ⊓|
            |

loose form   LF

example: L F
            ___

dwelling in the air   Dω

example: Dω
            ∧

flat-backed   —

example: =
           ⁄—

hollow-backed   ∪

example: ∪
           ___

propping at base of obstacle   ∧

example: ∧∧

twisting   T⍵

example: T⍵
            ∧

lying on side   L o S

example: L o S
              I

drifting in the air to left   ↖

example: ↑___

drifting in the air to right   ↗

example: ___↗

rail knocked down with any part
of horse's body in front of stifle   Ⓚ   placed to right of obstacle

example: ∧ Ⓚ

rail knocked down with
any part of horse's body   Ⓚ   placed to left of obstacle
behind stifle

example: Ⓚ —

rail touched with any part
of horse's body in front of stifle   •   placed to right of obstacle

example: — •

rail touched with any
part of horse's body behind stifle   •   placed to left of obstacle

example: • —

standard or wing knocked down
with any part of horse, rider,   S(K)
or equipment

example: ↖ S(K)

standard or wing touched
with any part of horse, rider, or equipment   S •

example: S •

FAULTS BETWEEN FENCES

propping on approach to obstacle   ⋀⋀

example: ⋀⋀⟍

breaking gait   (B)

example:
    horse breaks gait behind   (B÷)
    only, i.e., "skips"

cuts a corner of ring   ¢

not bent   — B

weaving on approach to fence   ⟩

example: ⟩ ⋀

bulging on approach to fence   )   or   (

                                bulges right   bulges left

                        each symbol placed to left of fence

example:) ___   or   (___

wrong lead (counter canter)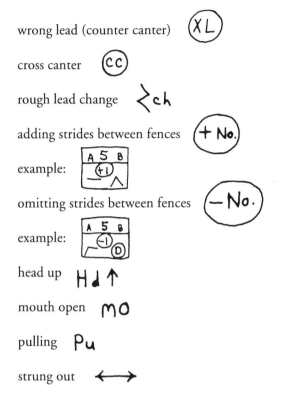

cross canter

rough lead change

adding strides between fences

example:

omitting strides between fences

example:

head up

mouth open

pulling

strung out

MANNERS AND WAY OF GOING

Pace

even pace (correct)   *E* v

slow pace   S l

fast pace   F s

erratic pace   E ʀ

Locomotion

excellent mover   E m

good mover   G m

fair mover   F m

poor mover   P m

General Impressions

If a horse habitually commits an error, such as holding its head in the air during a large part of the course, or has a major error, such as a refusal, this should be noted on the right side of the card, just after the box for the last fence.

EQUITATION SYMBOLS

Basic Symbols

toe   T

heel   H

leg   L g

seat   S

eye   I

head   H d

hand   H n

back   B k

rein   R n

stirrup   S t p

bad   B d

good   G d

short   S h

long   L N g

backward   ↰

forward   ↷

in (placed to right of word)   ←

example: L N ←   is "leans in"

out (placed to right of word)   →

example: T →   is "toes out"

up   ↑

down   ↓

weak   W к

strong   S t

rough   ⟩

smooth   S m o

loose   L s

stiff   S t f

little   X

very   V

not   —

lead   L d

diagonal   D g

Position in the Air

good position   Γ

perching   /

ducking   ∧

jackknifing   <

dropping back   D B

left in the air   Ⓛ

roached back   ⌒

swaybacked   ⌣

fixed hands   F H N

open hands   O H N

eyes down   I ↓

heel up   H ↑

toe out   T →

leg out   L g →

Position Between Fences

behind motion   B m

ahead of motion   A m

late eye
(looking too late to upcoming fence)   l a t e I

bad eye (poor timing to a fence)   B d I

leans for leads (leans to check leads on corners)   L L

leg off horse's side   ∧

Additional Faults

Other errors can be designated by using a combination of the above symbols. You can also use markings from the list of hunter symbols when necessary. For example, if a rider does not bend his horse around the corners of the ring, you would mark the error the same as you would during hunter classes: - B

INDEX

Anna Jane White-Mullin began riding when she was five years old, and was "discovered" by George Morris when she was eleven years old. Competing in major horse shows on the East Coast, Ms. White-Mullin won junior hunter and equitation championships at many noteworthy shows, including Ox Ridge, Fairfield, North Shore, Piping Rock, Harrisburg, Washington, Madison Square Garden, and the Florida Circuit shows. In 1971, coached by Ronnie Mutch, she won the Alfred B. Maclay Finals on her horse, Rivet, and was awarded a gold medal for winning twenty USET classes.

After graduating from Randolph-Macon Woman's College, Ms. White-Mullin continued her equestrian activities as a Registered (Big "R") judge in the hunter, hunter seat equitation, and jumper divisions. In 1986, she was a panelist at the AHSA's Hunter Seat Equitation Judges Clinic in San Francisco, presenting her slide show based on *Judging Hunters and Hunter Seat Equitation*. Subsequently, her slides were added to the permanent files of the AHSA.

Ms. White-Mullin serves as a judge, clinician, and lecturer throughout the North and South American continents. She is the author of *Winning: A Training and Showing Guide for Hunter Seat Riders*. She lives in Gadsden, Alabama, where she makes her home with her husband and two children on their farm, Bellerophon.

Other books from Trafalgar Square

CENTERED RIDING
Sally Swift

LUNGEING THE HORSE AND RIDER
Sheila Inderwick

RIDE WITH YOUR MIND
An Illustrated Masterclass in Right Brain Riding
Mary Wanless

THE RIDING TEACHER
The Basic Guide to Correct Methods of Classical Instruction
Alois Podhajsky

THAT WINNING FEELING!
A New Approach to Riding Using Psychocybernetics
Jane Savoie

WINNING
A Training and Showing Guide for Hunter Seat Riders
Anna Jane White-Mullin

For a complete catalog of Trafalgar Square equestrian books,
please write to:

Trafalgar Square Publishing
Box 257
North Pomfret, Vermont 05053